Rae

by Chelsea Rae Swiggett edited by Deborah Reber

Health Communications, Inc.
Deerfield Beach, Florida

www.hcibooks.com

Library of Congress Cataloging-in-Publication Data

Swiggett, Chelsea Rae.
   Rae : my true story of fear, anxiety, and social phobia /
Chelsea Rae Swiggett.
     p. cm.
   ISBN-13: 978-0-7573-1527-5
   ISBN-10: 0-7573-1527-5
   1. Swiggett, Chelsea Rae—Mental health.   2. Social phobia in
adolescence—Patients—Biography.   3. Anxiety in adolescence.
I. Title.
RJ506.S63S85 2010
618.92'852250092—dc22
[B]

                                            2010021677

Publisher: Health Communications, Inc.
          3201 S.W. 15th Street
          Deerfield Beach, FL 33442–8190

Cover design by Larissa Hise Henoch
Interior formatting by Dawn Von Strolley Grove

I'd like to dedicate this book
to my mom, who has put up with A LOT
and still manages to hold it all together
(while baking twenty pies simultaneously).
And to the rest of my family—my dad and stepmother,
who rock; my many Brady-Bunch-esque siblings;
and Emili, who's always been there for me.

Chapter I

THE CLICK OF MY VAN DOOR IS SIMILAR to the monotonous beeps of an alarm clock. You know how, after you've heard the same incessant noise day after day—always with the same dreaded awakening—you begin to cringe at the sound? That's what our van door, sliding open, does to me. It's the bugle of yet another school day.

Since I'm totally into mythology, I'll relate how I feel about school by referencing a well-known tale of a fellow named Sisyphus who, for doing something punishable to the gods, was forced to push an extremely heavy boulder up a hill day after day. Once he got to the top, the boulder would roll back down and he'd have to start all over again. School is my boulder. And I have *no* idea what I did to piss off Zeus.

I think it has less to do with school and more to do with the people occupying it. I'm, under no lesser terms, the opposite of a "people person." I'm a loner, and I like it that way. But humanity is kind of a nationwide epidemic, as any die-hard Buffy fan would quote, so I hobble myself down the sidewalk and into the glass doors of my high school.

I walk down the halls, watching my admittedly ugly tennis shoes clomp themselves over shiny tiles. I try to stay on one line as I make my way to my locker and on to homeroom. When I get to my seat and classes start, the evaluation begins. You know how people say you are your own toughest critic? It's totally true.

I zone out once the teacher starts talking, and the only thing I think about is how people view me. I check my breathing to make sure I can't be heard. I yank my shirt and pants so there's no way anyone can see an inch of me. I bite my lip and suffer through what I'm sure is just an assessment of how I look, cleverly disguised as "Homeroom."

Everything comes down to how I act, too. I know I'm quiet, but I'd rather go unnoticed than say something wrong and be insulted for it. Right now, I'm on the edge of my seat, waiting for my name to be called for attendance. Waiting, in dread, to speak out the word "here." When I quietly do, I wonder if I said it too silently or if my voice pitched awkwardly.

Everyone starts talking in whispers while the rest of the attendance is called. I hear everything I'd ever want to know about X's party or A's concert. People always talk like nobody's listening in. It's not like I eavesdrop on purpose, but if someone's having a conversation right next to a ghost, that poor ghost can't help but pick up a few disjointed words.

"The football game was . . ." "I can't believe she . . ." "Were you at . . . ?"

Sometimes I wonder what it'd be like to be someone else, like the girl two rows up and one seat over who had "an awesome time" this weekend. If we somehow pulled a *Freaky Friday* with our minds, would life be easier? I'm not naive enough to think other people don't have problems . . . we *all* do. But I know it'd be nice to not care so much. To just let things go and be happy and carefree.

I made a promise to myself that this year, my freshman year in high school, would be different. I moved from my last school in Berea to get a fresh start here at Avon Lake. I was done being labeled "mute," and I thought with a new school I could make myself over and be a new, outgoing person. As it turns out, it doesn't matter what school I'm at; I'm still chronically shy. While everyone else is busy talking like normal teenagers, I'm doodling. It's pretty depressing when someone who can't even draw a basic stick figure is resorting to "art" just to busy herself. There are lumps of mashed potatoes where my clouds are supposed to be.

The bell rings, and I'm five minutes closer to the end of the day. Welcome to my life.

* * *

Gym is one of the absolute *worst* parts of my life. I don't think it's just me, either, after listening to all the moans and complaints I hear during class. It's basically Hades' underworld domain for all the luckless uncoordinated kids. And, yes, I'd be included in that group.

To make matters worse, I've always been taller than average, and every single year when I get a new gym teacher, I'm told the exact same thing.

"You should play basketball!" They always say this with a raise of the eyebrows and an exaggerated smile. Like all it takes for someone to be talented in basketball is height. In that case, go attack Steve Urkel and see if *he* wants to shoot hoops.

But inevitably, right around the basketball unit, the pestering miraculously stops. I think it's because they've witnessed me moving in the opposite direction of the correct basket and swatting the ball openhanded one too many times.

Now that I'm at Avon Lake, we start off each gym class by running laps around the gymnasium. There's nothing worse than being alarmingly self-conscious and then adding sweat and shorts to the mix. I always wonder if it's normal to be this anxious about every step I take, if it's normal to consider every breath that comes out of my mouth. I feel like I'm Bambi—a newborn doe, struggling to walk without tripping. But, unlike Bambi, I don't ever get used to my own legs. I look around at my classmates and see the ease of walking and talking on their faces, like it's no big deal. But every twitch of my body, just like each word I speak, is something I analyze my worth over. And it seems like every gym class results in yet another humiliating and embarrassing scenario for me.

Like when we started doing the track unit. We'd have to run the mile, and I'd be panting and out of breath, dashing into the locker room to change in five seconds before sprinting to my next class, which was, until recently, sociology. I was actually really interested in taking the course, until I discovered I was the only freshman in the entire class. That's like being the only runt in a litter of adorable puppies. Plus, something about speeches came up early on in the semester, and I transferred straight out of that curriculum. They put me in business, which at most had one other freshman. It still sucked, but at least I didn't have to do much speaking.

One day, after doing laps in gym, I walked into business

class and sat in my assigned seat, dripping sweat.

"Did you just have gym?" the girl next to me asked.

"Yep," I whispered back.

"Were you outside?"

"Yeah."

"Oh, was it raining?"

"Uh, no. . . ." I said, confused about why she was asking.

"Oh."

After a moment, I realized she was asking because I was so sweaty she thought my perspiration was rainwater. I about died in my seat. If it was actually possible to croak from embarrassment, the Grim Reaper himself would have walked into my classroom at that exact moment, scythe ready to drag me down to the underworld. I think most people would laugh it off and forget about it an hour later, but I thought about it for weeks.

Another time I had gym, I was beyond late for business class, so I changed in a flurry. I was wearing a tank top under my shirt, being a fan of many layers. While I was rushing to class, I realized my tank seemed a lot longer than I originally thought it was. My clothes aren't usually in the habit of growing, so I was suspicious, but too hurried to do anything about it.

When I got to my seat, my shirt started slipping again. That's when I realized what was going on. In my rush to change, I had put both shirts on at the same time and the sleeves of the tank didn't actually make it on my shoulders. I waited for the teacher to pass out papers, and I looked around the classroom. Most heads were turned down, so I awkwardly popped my arms into my shirt and did a dance to rearrange my two shirts in the right order.

If anyone looked up at that moment, they would have seen me, arms in my shirt, wiggling around my limbs and looking like a gremlin in the process of deforming. My face was *beet* red.

Needless to say, gym was the hell to my hell, and I absolutely loathed it. But I tried. I ran when our teacher whistled. I crunched until I ached. I sat with my back against the wall in an invisible chair, legs yelling at me in flames. I wore the ridiculous Avon Lake shorts and T-shirts every day, sneakers ready to squeak across the floor. I shouldered my embarrassment while in the locker room, stripping in the company of a freaky amount of skinny, waiflike teenagers. At the very beginning of the school year, when my "fresh start" was still in mind, I did everything the shrilling whistle asked of me.

But today, I don't want to dress. I don't want to run miles, gasping for breath and sweating through my shirt. I don't want to go through the whole oops-my-top-is-falling-off scenario again, or trip and fall on my face. I just want to be alone, by myself, playing on my dorky imaginary farm in *Harvest Moon* (a mind-numbing video game that's infinitely more fun than school). I don't want people to see me, and I *definitely* don't want people to see me running around like a sweaty chicken. So I just . . . don't dress. It's a dramatic moment for me, because I've always been a straight-A student. I've always done what I'm told and aimed to please, my head tucked down and a pencil in my hand. So when I walk out in my jeans and T-shirt, sitting down at my assigned spot on the floor, it's with a taste of rebellion. My gym teacher asks why I'm not in uniform, like I committed some kind of felony.

"I forgot my clothes at home," I lie. I've always been a

convincing liar, which probably isn't something to brag about. I'll tell my family ridiculous whoppers, like a bat landed on my shoulder or that I saw a tiger running loose on the baseball field, convincing everyone to be gullible before I laugh and expose my joke. That sounds viciously evil, but it's kind of like April Fools' Day 365 times a year. It's funny to me, and it's made me a damn good liar. So, when I look my gym teacher in the face and tell him that I forgot my clothes, it's convincing, even though I know they're hiding out in my locker as I say it. I get a zero for the day, but I'm excused from gym. And, in the end, that's all that really matters.

Sometimes, I wish I could just be excused from *life*. Maybe not life, technically—I'm not suicidal—but at least the *demands* of life. You have to go to school, you have to be smart, you have to be pretty, you have to be thin, you have to do what you're told, and then you have to grow up. I wish I could just pull a Peter Pan and fly around in Never Never Land as a forever-youthful child.

Chapter 2

I'M NOT EXACTLY SURE WHEN my social awkwardness first began, but I know I've always had a hard time fitting in. My brain seemed to refuse normality and accepted a religion of loner-ism instead.

* * *

"We have a new student today, class," my fourth-grade teacher said, pointing to a desk near mine. The girl next to me smiled, and I became friends with her for mainly one reason. "Her name is Chelsea," Ms. Glotzbecker finished.

"My name's Chelsea, too!" I remember saying excitedly,

toothy grin in place. Back then, it seemed like the coolest, most fateful thing to have ever happened to me. Thankfully, our mothers chose the same name, or I might not have opened my mouth at all. It turns out, though, that both of us had the same personality: frighteningly goofy.

I was a chubby kid. I had those little baby cheeks aunts love to pinch, but like the Christmas sweaters those cheek-pinching aunts usually gift, I was a few years too old for them. My cheeks didn't fit. Matched with a muffin top, I was basically Teletubby offspring. Except (hopefully) less creepy. Chelsea, on the other hand, had a full head of curly hair and a strong personality that made her seem completely sure of herself. Though I've never had that confidence, she knew who she was, and I admired that.

But our differences didn't matter. Chelsea and I would stay up late at night, throwing our hair up in buns on top of our heads and carrying around a coffee pot, singing our own made-up song about being little Scottish girls. We'd play pranks on everyone who was sleeping, like the time we took a bottle of orange soda and poured some of it on my older brother's head. I remember when we woke up the next morning there was a bright orange stain on his scalp. Other times, we'd sneak out at night, jumping from my window to the ground in one big leap, to pick flowers.

But Chelsea could be outgoing anywhere and in any situation, whereas I could only be myself at home. I could only be fully comfortable when I was surrounded by familiarities. I can't relax if I'm in a restaurant or at the park or in the library. I can't relax if I'm around my cousin's friend or my friend's cousin. I have to know the place I'm in and the people I'm around, or I'm just a ball of nerves. I'm an introvert. But Chelsea wasn't. And, as outgoing people are prone to do, she quickly became "popular."

After a few months of hanging out with Chelsea, I realized what it meant to be bullied. The people Chelsea hung around with took every second of the day to stab my heart out, *Mean Girls*-style. Excluding Chelsea, it was a vicious group. Most of the day, they'd criticize me and bash me until I was a metaphorical pulp sitting dejectedly on the blacktop concrete. I was an easy target; I was quiet, and I didn't fight back. I just sat there and endured it, day after day, while I was berated.

Most kids spend their day waiting for recess, the time of day where you could run free, climb on metal, and swing until your feet hit the sky. But I dreaded it, because it also meant a lack of restriction. There were no teachers in close enough range for ears to grab brutal words.

"Look at her! Her stomach just *bulges* out!"

"Seriously, try and suck in."

And, my favorite—when I was invited to a pool party: "You won't wear a two-piece, right?" The pathetically sad part was that I was so excited to be invited I just smiled and said no.

Despite this petty mocking, I never stood up to them. They threw their insults at me, one at a time, waiting for one of them to cut me so they could watch me bleed. I felt strong that I was stoic, never showing them their jibes actually stung me. Sometimes I laughed, sometimes I shouldered it, and sometimes I just shut my mouth. I never cried. Until one day, I did.

"She has rolls! Look! Her sides, like, go over her pants!" I looked down at some of my pudgy fat and took a deep intake of breath. "Here, stand next to me and look how much fatter she is." One of those nonswallowable bumps lodged into my throat, and I fought back to keep from tearing up. "Look how fat she looks! Oh, my God."

There were so many things I wish I would have said to earn me at least an ounce of dignity, but I didn't. Instead, I walked over to sit by myself on the swings and cried out the water I drank for lunch. After recess ended, I heard Chelsea talking to her friends while I sat in my seat.

"You made her cry," she told them.

The girl looked back at me and asked if it was true. "Did you really *cry?*"

"No," I said in a shaky voice, but my eyes were too watery to back up my lie.

Our teacher started handing out worksheets, and I was beyond ashamed that anyone else saw me while I was vulnerable. I flipped my hair over my face and started scratching on my paper.

Those mindless scratches led to a realization—I'd never

really fit in. Not just with these kinds of girls, but with *anyone*. It's either eat or be eaten in this society, and everyone has a voracious appetite. The only person you can really trust not to make a meal out of you is yourself; even cannibals don't stoop *that* far. It's just me against the world. It's a pretty depressing realization.

* * *

Maybe it was because of this realization that by fifth grade—after years of seeing eccentric behavior mocked—I became what I hated. A mean girl.

I'd made friends with a couple of kids in my class, and we'd spend recess sharing gossip or laughing about other people; it felt glorious to finally belong somewhere. We never lacked girls to practice our arsenal of insults on, our bows notched and a relentless game of archery always at the ready. That year, there were two girls in particular who were a little beyond strange, and, unfortunately, they became my targets and I became the arrow. Monkey see, monkey do.

One of these two "Weird Girls" (WGs) had stringy,

greasy hair that led to our scrunched noses. My friends and I would constantly ask her if she showered, while laughing in her face. We were the *Heathers* of the twenty-first century and we were rarely in a relenting mood. One day, we came in from recess and one of the WGs put a stick on her desk.

"What's *that*?" I asked, pointing to the branch lying on her table. I looked over to my friend, and we both raised our eyebrows.

"My wand," she said. This was, understandably, hilarious to us. We snickered over it for a while, and when WG left our vicinity, I whispered over to one of my friends, "Go throw it in the trash." She obligingly got up, broke the stick in half, and threw it into the garbage. We all grinned conspiratorially.

The WG came back and, after frantically searching for her wand, found it in the trash. That's where things got bad. Laughably bad. She ran to the teacher. "They threw my stick away!" she said, with a stomp of her foot and a point in our direction. This probably would have had more impact if it wasn't, you know, a *stick*.

"We thought it was garbage," we replied, even though, to her, we knew it wasn't. Obviously, we didn't get in trouble for throwing away a stick, even one with magically powered bark. But, looking back, it wasn't about whether or not we got in "trouble." This girl had an imagination, no matter how weird it was. I had one before, too. But I had people who crushed mine, and so I crushed others to pay back for it—metaphorical blood for blood. It wasn't my most prideful year, but at least it was socially educational.

* * *

I watch a girl walking into my ninth-grade classroom with a Care Bear sticking out of her pocket, but I keep my mouth closed. Actually, I do that a lot these days, regardless of how weird the person is.

Back in the day, in the Middle East, criminals would be punished by having their tongues cut out and fed to the king's cat. Some believe that the phrase "cat got your tongue" originated from this history, but it's not back in the day and I'm not in the Middle East, so I really have no excuse. Otherwise, I'd probably go mug a noble or something just so I wouldn't have to feel like such a freak.

I can only imagine it. "Oh, her? She doesn't have a tongue. Otherwise, she'd tooootally talk to you. No big deal." Yeah, completely plausible. But, in reality, whenever anybody says anything to me, I just freeze up and glare or something, like a thoughtless automaton.

Chapter 3

"LUNCHTIME!" THE BELLS TOLL. They might as well chime "awkward!" because that's all lunch really is to me. I take my seat next to several complete strangers plus my stepsister, who I always socially latch onto because I feel too pathetic sitting by myself. I sit, nearly invisible, and watch everyone talk while I pick my hangnails.

My stomach grumbles, and I'm automatically red-cheeked thinking anyone heard it, but satisfied that my hunger acknowledges itself. I sit without food in front of me, like usual. If I'm offered a chip or two, I'll take them. But I usually forgo breakfast and lunch, coming home and eating as little as possible before going to bed. There are too many skinny people in Avon Lake to do otherwise.

As usual, I ignore any moments where my thoughts could be spoken out loud like a normal teenager. Were I normal, I might have chimed in about the way my second-period teacher spits when he talks or the movie I saw last week or the shows I'm watching. But I'm not normal, so I don't say anything at all. Silence is my first language and English is my second. I've sat with these people for around two months, and I know every single one of them would be completely shocked if I ever interjected. I am beyond silence.

While I sit there, listening to people talk about whatever their little mouths can spew, I realize my life is complete shit. The only person I spend time with every day is my cat, Kringer. Or possibly Mr. Darcy from *Pride and Prejudice*. This is a disturbing line only hermits or bag ladies can understand. I realize, with a horrible fascination, that my future can only lead to one path: I'm fated to be a "Crazy Cat Lady" (CCL). I'll have fifty stray tabbies in my home, litter boxes next to my bed, and gray hair that frizzes and sheds, much like the cats I'll house. It's a depressing thought. But where else do I fit in?

Not with *these* people, harmlessly chatting to each other about clothes and spontaneity. Not with the people at the table two rows behind with studs in their eyes and belted pants. Not with the group across the cafeteria that speaks "Laughter" like a first language. I'm just a stubborn, soggy puzzle piece whose edges now refuse to click with the rest. Sure, I'm not the only rebellious puzzle piece, but the other ones don't seem to inspire clicking, either. Those stupid edge pieces have it so easy.

At least I'll be a skinny *Cat Lady,* I think, watching everyone put food into their mouths and keeping mine shut. One of these days, I'll drop to a size two and everything will be 90 percent better. Or maybe I'll just join the circus and become a mime. They're *supposed* to be silent, right? I can paint my own imaginary box and stick myself in it. I can live in an imaginary house and play imaginary Monopoly with my imaginary friends. I can eat imaginary food and live an imaginary life.

I launch myself into my own mind and escape this fickle thing called reality.

* * *

I reach Spanish class and can already tell it's a game day. There are words written on the board and a slaphappy hand waiting on a tabletop. My Spanish teacher is really cool—we have these days that we spend playing games to help us memorize words like *el gato* and *la casa*. They're fun, but I hate when it's my turn to play. Okay, it's a little weird to say a game is fun and that you hate playing it. I'm aware of that. But I despise when attention is on me, like with presentations or answering questions. Getting up in front of a board and slapping a little plastic faux hand around on it (which is what one of said games entails) causes attention.

Today's excitement? Bubbles. My teacher splits us into two teams and chooses one representative of each team as "Designated Bubble Blowers" (DBBs). Luckily, I'm not one of them. In this game, each member of our team has to conjugate verbs before all the bubbles pop. I sit in the back, hoping I'll somehow be skipped over.

The girl next to me starts talking to the guy in front of

us while we wait to conjugate. He has long bushy hair and rides his bike everywhere around town. I've seen him come to school with big sweat stains on the back of his shirt. I mean, really, how much can you love your bike? He's like Lance Armstrong or something.

So, of course, his bike riding comes up.

"You live by me," the girl says. "If you bike to school every day, how the hell do you get here on time? It's so far away."

"Leprechauns," he replies.

"Uuh . . . ?"

"My bike is powered by leprechauns."

"Like, the little green dudes?"

"Yeah, the car companies just don't want you to know about it."

His face is completely straight. This guy has some serious mental issues. What. The. Hell. I start laughing uncontrollably, putting my head on my desk and trying to cover my face. But it's one of those moments where laughing is the only thing you can do, and you can't even hold a breath because it's all expelling into gurgling hiccups.

"Chelsea," my Spanish teacher says, interrupting my hysterics. "Can you blow the bubbles?"

"Uh, sure," I whisper. *No. No, no, no, no, no, no, no.* I walk to the front of the room and avoid everyone's eyes on me. I dip the wand in the bubble batter and blow. Nothing happens. I attempt try number two. Dip, blow, nothing. Rinse and repeat. When you fail at blowing bubbles, I think the universe is sending you a unanimous message: you suck.

I let out a laugh and look to my teacher nervously. "I can't do it," I say, and she calls someone else to take my place. I check to make sure she doesn't give me a zero for bad bubble blowing.

Making my way back to my desk is like a walk of shame. I plop down on the prickly plastic of my seat and will the conjugating to restart. I know I won't care about this in a few days, but right now I feel like I do after every moment attention is unwillingly cast on me: revoltingly embarrassed. I wish I could be the type of person who isn't bothered by something like unblown bubbles, but I'm not. I'm my own type of person.

I'm the type of person who gets embarrassed—not just red-faced embarrassed, but moments of utter humiliation where I feel like every person in the room is watching, staring, criticizing, laughing, and generally hating me—over things like: a) breathing, b) eating, c) walking, and d) *being*. The type of things normal people do so easily give me more trouble and embarrassment than you can imagine. When I walk down the hall, I wonder if my walk is straight on or if I curve to the right or if my stomach jiggles or if my shirt is laying right. When I sit in a classroom, I wonder if my breathing is uneven, so I try to slow it down and then end up with a lack of breath so I have to yawn. And then I wonder if anyone saw my face distort from that yawn, and I get worried and even *more* mortified. I hate being this type of person, if it even is a type. Maybe I'm my own species, bound to eternal embarrassment day after day.

I picture myself painting an imaginary hole across the shiny, cracked tiles and dropping straight into oblivion. This mime occupation is looking more appealing every single second.

* * *

I open the doors to my school and walk out onto the sidewalk. Step. Step. Step. The click of our van door opening after school is a beautiful, joyful sound. It's weird that a particular sound can be both loathsome and lovesome, but it's the truth. Right now, it means I can go home. For about fifteen hours, that is. I feel bad that Sisyphus never got this kind of reprieve.

"Hi, honey. How was school?" my mom asks with a smile on her face as she puts the van in drive.

"Fine," I grunt. For some reason, people always feel the need to say they're fine when they're not. It's hardwired into our DNA to pretend we're happy. Your neighbors could have just lost their daughter or your cousin could be getting beat up by her father, and you wouldn't know. Because they'd smile and say they're fine. What *is* it with our society that makes us present an exterior that completely contradicts the interior? I can't answer that, but I can follow it. *I'm fine. School was just . . . fine.* But it's not. It's really, really not. From the minute I walk into that hellish building every day, down to the minute I walk out, I'm wishing I'm somewhere else. I'm *Ripley's Believe It or Not's* biggest ball of nerves. We chug along to our house, passing white stuccos and townhouses where all the people living inside are perfectly fine.

Chapter 4

11:00 PM—I CAN'T SLEEP. Every time I close my eyes I think about tomorrow. I think about death. I think about life. I think about religion. I think about thinking. I think entirely too much, and my brain refuses to shut off.

11:30 PM—I hear a low-flying plane, and my heart beats way too fast. I think about it bombing us, or ramming into our house. I'm convinced I'm going to die. The sound of it flying over our house, rumbling the roof, is more than I can take, and I have to plug my ears. My heart's palpitating, and I can feel it dance in my chest. It feels like it's doing somersaults in my rib cage, spinning 360 degrees before thumping two obnoxiously loud beats and twirling again. My stamina is in overdrive. I'm having a panic attack.

12:00 AM—I toss off the covers and try to read. My eyes droop and I set my book on the nightstand, pulling my blanket back over my head.

12:15 AM—Another plane. Another panic attack. I think about death some more.

12:45 AM—I finally sleep, but not peacefully. The half of my body and brain that isn't asleep knows I'll be pushing the boulder up that hill again in the morning.

6:00 AM—Coffee.

As I drink my caffeine, asleep to the world, I inwardly hate my heart. This is what every night for me is like: filled with thoughts and worry about death, destruction, and chaos. Loud sounds always inspire panic to raid my mind, attacking it with the vigor of a Spartan warrior. I mean, I know the chances are slim that the plane flying overhead is filled with terrorists or that the loud booming noises in the background are nuclear bombs. I know the planes are full of harmless passengers and the booms are probably fireworks or thunder, both natural and explainable things. But it doesn't matter. Logic is missing from my mind, and

I can't be rational with fear. It takes control and leaves me in a heap of blankets, closing my eyes tight and biting my lip so hard it bleeds.

The absolute worst? Thunderstorms. It's not the lightning that scares me, even though that's the only dangerous part. It's the thunder. The pounding of God's fists rapping on our house and rattling my bones. I can feel thunder coming before it hits, and it jolts me with every rumble. If the storm lasts an hour, I'll be in complete fear every second of those sixty minutes. I've spent hours huddled in the bathroom at night, away from windows, trying to escape the noise and subsequent fear.

And then there are road trips. On long rides, I wake up every half hour from nightmares about crashes and metal. It sucks, because I really love our family vacations. Each one of them is this hugely memorable experience, yet whenever I go back and muse on them, I always try and block the vehicle part entirely out of the vacation. I have this idea that I love road trips, and sometimes I really do. It's fun to be in a car with someone and chat, and it's fun to make pit stops for iced tea or chips. But the highway? Not fun. I'm not fond of being in a huge chunk of metal, hauling ass at sixty miles an hour. To me, it's like walking on a tightrope. Driving is pretty damn dangerous, and because of that, I'm afraid to take a single step. When I get to the end of the rope, I'm relieved, but I know I'll have to walk back again.

I used to try to hype up the road trips in my mind before we left. For long trips, we would typically leave really early in the morning, around 5:00 AM, since my mom and stepdad are naturally early risers. "Early" was generally taboo for me, so I'd usually stay up until we left, preferring to be unconscious the entire ride. A couple of my siblings had the same idea, so we'd make coffee and watch movies, our eyes drooping before we forced them back open.

Even though I hated unwanted insomnia, I absolutely loved staying up for a purpose. Most nights, my role was this: tossing, turning, counting, meditating. My role was to try to sleep, and my role was to fail miserably. So when a night came around where lack of sleep would actually be *useful*, my night-owl tendencies called to me. It was *fun*. It was a part of the whole vacation thing. I really liked packing all my stuff and loading it in the van, setting out for a new adventure. I always felt like I was Indiana Jones or something, stowing my provisions and setting out to find something new. The only sucky part was the actual driving. When we got on that highway, excitement was generally replaced with fear. Excitement, fear. Excitement, fear. Excitement, fear. For me, long trips are like bipolar, adrenaline-filled nightmares.

One time, when we went on a family vacation to Ocean City, New Jersey, I had panic attacks the entire ride there. I had this fear we'd get in a car accident and fall into the ocean, trapped in our stupid red van. I pictured all seven of us drowning, flailing our arms as our car plummeted down, down, down.

Having a panic attack is something completely internal—it's a strong jolt of pure terror, making your heart palpitate and roll around in your chest—but it makes you feel as if you are externally crawling out of your skin. It takes a lot of power not to curl up in the fetal position and weep your fear out, which is what I wanted to do almost every second of that car trip. An attack makes you sweat and shake and just . . . *panic*.

I remember when we got back home, I made my mom go online and order some kind of car-window-breaking device in case we ever got trapped underwater. I remember asking my dad the best way to escape—should I try and cut a hole in the top of the car with a pocket knife? Should I throw something heavy at the window? I tried to logically think of every situation that could happen and every way I could get out of it. But panic attacks create a fear so strong that reason is completely lost and your veins bleed pure terror.

It was a great vacation, though. There was one day we walked out to the beach and it was *completely* covered with jellyfish. There wasn't even a single patch of safe sand to put your towel on, because every few square feet had a sea buddy waiting to tan with you. It was crazy how many there were, as if they all cloned themselves fifty times over and then reproduced. We had dolphins swimming 100 feet away from us, and we smelled like salt and sand every day. We sat out on our balconies and relaxed, our feet propped up on the railing and wind in our sea-breezed hair.

But before long, we were in the car again, driving home. Drives home are always worse than the drive there. Less excitement, but the same amount of fear. On our way back from this particular trip, there was a holdup. For about five hours. Finally, an officer came walking through the parked cars and whispered into windows.

"Sorry, folks," the officer said. "There was a car crash. Fatalities." I noticed the plural.

If we had left even ten minutes earlier, would we have been in that crash? Would we have been one of those plurals? Were there children in the car? Did a family lose their father, their mother, their son? Who were the survivors? What did the car behind them see? If we hadn't stopped to get breakfast, would one of use be dead? If, if, if? Who, what, when, where, how?

I think I was even *more* terrified of cars after that.

See, fear is a big part of my life. It's what I go to sleep with, wake up with, and live with. Sometimes, it just needs to mind its own damn business and let me live.

I remember hearing that if you think about death all the time, you're at risk for suicide. But what about people who think about fear all the time? I think about death a lot, but I don't *want* it. I fear it with an abnormal passion. Am I obsessed with life, then? Am I at risk for overdosing on *being*? I wish I didn't have to go through life fearing death at each corner, but it's inescapable. I *will* die. I don't know when or how, but I will. And that terrifies me so much that I fear life. Most of all, I fear fear.

Chapter 5

ONE HOUR OF SLEEP. This time, it was on purpose.

"Mom? I don't feel so good," I say, putting on a face that I'm hoping looks very, very sickly. It involves scrunched eyebrows and a perfected pout. I'm a certified expert at pretending to be sick. I should have a plaque.

I decide to put these skills to use today because even the thought of heading to school sucks my energy dry. I mean, it's not like I'm gleeful to go to school on *any* day, but today? I'm tired and I'm grumpy, and if I have to go to school again I might have a mental breakdown. Over and over and over again, I put on a face that says it'll be okay and then spend eight hours realizing it won't be. I try and convince myself that everything will be fine, but every minute I spend around other people convinces me that I'm not. It's a game of catch-22 I constantly play with myself. If I keep acting normal, I hope one day I will be, but every time I try, I just let myself down. I picture myself socializing at some random party, but when I get there I just end up sitting in the corner by myself. I'm *so* entirely sick of this game.

Plus, I didn't do my biology assignment. That's not entirely a rare thing these past few weeks, but this one's worth a heap of my grade. Lately, I've been skipping math assignments and science worksheets like they're optional, and it's bitten me in the ass. So I decide that today is as good a day as any to take a break. And, I mean, it's not like I'm lying. I really *am* sick. Not from the flu, a cold, or the plague, as I overdramatically claim. I'm just plain sick of people. I wish there was something I could do to remedy that, but the only thing I can think of doing, currently, is hiding my head under the covers and giving up.

Today, like on most days I claim to be sick, my mom feels my head, which I warmed up under the blankets before she came downstairs. Getting an hour of sleep automatically makes you look like complete shit, so it definitely helps my case. This is another prime example of the rewards you reap from being a talented liar.

Come to think of it, there was only one time I had actually been sick in the past few years. Once, in seventh grade, I woke up with flames in my throat and a voice that sounded like an eighty-year-old chain smoker. The 'rents said to try and go to school anyway, since I'd played sick a week or two before. Looking back, it's kind of ironic how often I faked being sick, because I actually seem to have a really good immune system. (Thanks, white blood cells!) Anyway, on this particular day in seventh grade, I grudgingly went to school, forgetting it was picture day.

When I got to class, I told my history teacher that I felt like death, but he advised me to wait until the click-click of the camera shutter, if I could possibly survive until then. What if I had actually died during pictures? Keeled over right there, captured in memory by a Canon? I'm sure he'd feel like a right ol' asshole. But I went into the bathroom and threw on some eyeliner anyway.

I know *everyone* hates their own school pictures, but I feel like I had a special right to complain. Under normal circumstances, I blame the photographers. They brush our hair in ridiculous ways, as if all of us hadn't spent the past half an hour trying to tame it ourselves, and tell us to tilt our head sideways. What the hell is *up* with that? But seriously, imagine having a 102-degree fever, the croak of a frog, and the disheveled appearance of a street bum—and then being forced to smile. Result equals not pretty. I went to the nurse the second they threw away that stupid black comb.

Of course, the nurse sent me home. I suffered all weekend, watching my stepmom stencil the walls with olive green paint. I only ever get sick when I can't benefit from it, so, of course my one dose of actual sickness would be during a weekend. It's a big cosmic joke. "Ha," says the world. It says that a lot.

So, right now, when I cough and pretend to be sick, I'm actually feeling 100 percent fine, if a little tired. When my mom calls me out of school, I pass out and sleep for hours, dreaming about sugarplum fairies and giant tsunamis. I wake up around 8:00 PM and get online, reading fan fiction until 6:00 in the morning, when I fake, yet again, a rough cough and a mild case of the sniffles.

Day after day, for the entire week, I fake sickness. I think I fake so good that my body actually *becomes* sick, because on day five, something happens. I'm eating a bowl of cereal and typing away at my computer when all of a sudden the cereal comes back up. It didn't even give me a fair warning. At least be considerate, stomach. "Hey, Chels, you're about to spew. Go to the bathroom." That's really all I ask. But I upchuck right there at my computer. The vomit sinks into my console, and I know no amount of keyboard duster will clean it out. I call my mom in and she picks up the keyboard, tilting it sideways. Watching my chunky cereal drain from between the keys and into a puddle on the counter makes me gag again. If I had anything else in my stomach, I'm sure it would have joined the rest of the alphabet pooled on the desk.

It was *weird*. Like, supernatural weird. I tell my body I'm sick all week, and it reacts. I'm probably telepathic or something cool like that.

My mom says, pretty rudely but fairly, that if I miss school another day, I have to go to the doctor. Even though I know I'm not sick, I say I'll go anyway. I'd rather face a doctor with absolutely no symptoms than walk into school again. I wonder what his diagnosis will be . . . chronic people-hate?

When I get to the doctor's office, they poke and test and drain my blood. They say I have nothing wrong with me, but they write me an "excused" note for school anyway. My mom has to pay for the visit, and I feel only slightly guilty.

Pretty soon, it's the weekend. I know that, barring death or a sudden case of the chicken pox, I'll have to deal with school again next week. No matter how much time I spend willing time to stop, tomorrow always comes. I'll have to carry my massive biology project into school, a week late, and deal with getting all of my missing assignments. It's going to be horribly embarrassing dragging the project to my classroom. Of course, it's the absolute farthest room from the front door. You have to go upstairs, hop over flaming coals, and pass through a labyrinth of white-walled corners to get there. And my project isn't the most delightful thing to see in the morning. I basically taped bags of decayed vegetables onto a board. Seriously. I was testing biodegradable foods and materials, so I dug a hole and filled it with corn (which I think an animal dug up and ate), apples, rubber bands, and all that good stuff. It was a half-assed attempt at science, and you could definitely tell.

On Monday, I'm holding my huge, decaying project with my forearms, struggling to get into school, when someone opens the door for me. I don't see who it is, and I barely mumble "thank you" under my breath before scuttling off. Someone being nice is normally enough to make me run.

Even though my note says "excused," it's horrible having to face my teachers and claim I've been sick again. I've held tens of little paper slips before, the box next to "unexcused absence" checked off by the school secretary. It's protocol to show these slips to teachers after missing school, and I dread it every single time. They probably think I'm either a) faking or b) have some kind of horrendous disease, like leprosy. Neither of those options makes me feel very good. I have to show my slip to each teacher and stand at the front of the classroom, waiting for my missed assignments to be handed to me, while everyone else sits in their seats and watches, probably debating whether leprosy is contagious. It makes me want to fake sick again tomorrow.

Chapter 6

BEING EXTREMELY SELF-CONSCIOUS, I'm always trying to improve myself. I look at myself in the mirror like I'm looking at an essay I'm trying to edit. I do it scientifically. If I have a bit of acne, I'll use acne creams religiously, almost like I'm erasing excess commas. If I think my butt's looking a little big, I skip a meal, almost like I'm shortening run-on sentences. If my hair is looking frizzy, I'll run it over with a straightening iron, almost like I'm rewording awkward word usage. But it's not just a dab of makeup here and a straightening of my shirt there. It's not just correcting grammar mistakes to bump myself up a percentage. It never stops. I turn self-improvement into a project that I'm constantly working on.

* * *

We live about an hour away from Cedar Point, home of the largest roller coaster in the United States. It's probably not the best place to live for someone with a massive fear of death and an overly active imagination. And, I mean, it's Ohio, so there's not much else to do. You're stuck going to the movies, painting your toenails, or hopping in a car headed toward Cedar Point. There's rarely an option four. And during Halloween, Cedar Point isn't content with huge-ass, stomach-dropping roller coasters everywhere. They add in ghosts. And haunted houses.

Don't get me wrong—I *love* haunted houses. For someone who hates fear, I actually love to be scared. I can read Stephen King books all day, and my favorite director is Tim Burton (although he's more morbid than scary). I think it's because I know the fright is artificial. I know the people are paid to jump out at you; and even though I scream when a scythe flashes in front of my face, it's not like they're actually murderers waiting to play with my entrails or eat my ears.

What gets an *actual*, certifiable adrenaline boost of fear is being stupid enough to get on a roller coaster flying at 10,000 miles an hour and reaching so high in the air the heavens try to grab you. I wish I knew a team of psychologists who could help me understand why the hell people love to be scared. Is it to test your bravery? To have a feeling of survival? Every time I'm on a roller coaster, I absolutely loathe it. I want it to end with each second, screaming and crying and squeezing my eyes shut so hard they pop. The minute it's over, though, I say the exact same thing I do every other time.

"Want to go again?"

It's stupid. I must be *really* masochistic. The reality is, I hate the feeling of fear, but I like the feeling of having felt it. That rush of "I'm okay" that settles over me is impossible to describe but utterly addicting. I spend so much time worrying about when I'll die that when I feel a rush of being alive, I'll hold onto it and beg to ride the coaster again.

Today, the Saturday before Halloween, we're going to Cedar Point.

"I'm *not* riding any roller coasters," I tell my friend Chelsea when I see some of the huge steel death traps in the distance threatening to touch the clouds. We're crossing a bridge with another ten minutes of driving ahead of us, but I can already see the coasters taunting me.

"Yes, you are." I'm starting to think this was a bad idea.

Once there, I'm immediately dragged to the Blue Streak, a wooden coaster that seems to be the smallest one in sight. Wood coasters make the creepiest noises, slowly cranking and creaking you up a hill before pulling you into a turn. But this one's small, as Chelsea blatantly points out, so I agree. Plus, the guy manning it is totally hot. He checks my seatbelt before the roller coaster starts. I drool.

As soon as the ride starts, I figure out why they call it the Blue Streak—because anyone watching the ride from below would see only that. This thing is *fast*. Tears leak out of my eyes from the wind, and I have to wipe them off by the time it stops. There are dead bugs on my shirt. Ew.

"I'm done!" I tell Chelsea as soon as we step down the stairs. Thankfully, it starts to rain, so she doesn't argue, and we speedily head off to mix with murderers. Haunted houses don't move, so they win over coasters any day. Besides, they're safer. I remember hearing a story about a boy who got his legs cut off on the Superman ride. A stray cable just up and chopped them off, like a demonic snake. I'm thinking whoever told me that story should have kept their mouth shut.

We meet two guys in line, and they decide to follow us in. I don't object, because it's always better to have some muscle when you're being chased by Jason or Michael Myers. Turns out they scream like little girls though, so they aren't too helpful.

We get to the end, and a foam alien is standing in the corner. I've absolutely hated aliens ever since I saw the movie *Dreamcatcher*. It's kind of hard not to be opinionated about aliens when you've seen them crawling out of people's stomachs. One of the guys reaches out and pokes its foam belly, thinking it's fake. It's not. It jumps out at us, and we ruin our tonsils with high-pitched yells.

I haven't eaten anything all day, and I'm pretty proud of myself about this. My stomach is grumbling so loudly it matches the rumbling of thunder the rain clouds have brought along. Chelsea buys some nachos, and I eat a few.

Earlier, before we drove to Cedar Point, Chelsea brought over a bottle of rum, currently hidden behind some clothes in my closet at home. She had this idea that we should starve the day away so the alcohol would hit us harder when we drank it later. I guess she was afraid we didn't have enough rum to actually get us drunk or something unless we were drinking on an empty stomach. I went along with her plan because it gave me another excuse not to eat, which was especially important if I was going to drink pointless calories later.

"I can't believe we ate!" Chelsea says after there are only a couple crumbs left in the basket of chips. "It wasted all our hard work today." That statement bothers me more than she knows. I feel an incredible wave of guilt for eating, and I imagine each chip floating around in my stomach.

"What, you guys don't eat when you want to lose weight or something? Why don't you just *exercise*?" one of the guys asks in a mocking way. I want to slap him across the face, even though it's a good question. Too bad I can't answer it.

Chelsea rehashes "our" idea to him, and the case is dropped. The gavel is banged, the judge stands up, and the witnesses leave the court. But the accused still has jail time to face.

Chelsea and I leave, go home, and drink ourselves silly. I'm happy when I throw it all up in the morning.

* * *

Skipping meals is just one of many methods I've used to control my weight. There are also the revoltingly disgusting Slim-Fast bars, which I manage to shove down my throat for breakfast, lunch, and dinner. Sure, the first few times you try and eat these evil demon bars, they don't taste too bad. They do have chocolate in them, after all. But when you make your diet revolve around them, eventually the thought of putting another bite in your mouth makes you gag worse than a bout of the flu.

I think my gag reflex is even more fluent for Slim-Fast bars than it is for broccoli. Not that I'm against greens, being a vegetarian, but ever since the "Meal Worm Incident" (MWI), where my entire family stumbled upon a family of meal worms in the fresh stalks of broccoli we were dining on one night, I can't look at them the same.

"Extra protein!" my dad had said. *Extra vomit*, I thought.

Anyway, I'm not sure why I'd continue to eat something I hate so much, but I've eaten more Slim-Fast bars than I would care to count. They only have 220 calories, and they fill you up with whatever the hell kind of chemicals are in them. These days, I've been eating about three of a day, equaling 660 total calories. Plus, with exercise, I figure I'll keep losing weight until I'm happy. I've already lost about ten pounds since the start of school, and I hope I can lose ten more. And then maybe ten more.

I slip up every now and then, eating something calorific like a slice of pizza. It makes me feel disgusting, but I sternly get back on track and shove more demons in my stomach. I hate when I eat, but I love the wait between meals, spending my time reading or watching movies to get my mind off of food and hunger. I crave getting hungry like a starving kid would crave food or an addict would crave their addiction. In a weird way, not eating gives me merit. If I spend my day doing nothing, I still feel accomplished. I feel as if tomorrow means something to me, instead of today being one more wasted step toward death.

I know that I get thinner with each day I diet—each second—and it makes me have more hope for the future. I imagine myself skinnier, at the beach hanging out with a group of friends or in a cute dress in some foreign country, being carefree. I figure things will start getting better once my image improves. I figure I can talk to people more easily if I'm pretty.

It's a vicious thing, my life.

Chapter 7

THERE IS THIS GIRL WHO SITS across from me in history. She seems a little strange, but, hey, the entire *class* is strange, including our teacher. Mr. Griffi uses these old, decrepit claws of dead animals as pointers for the board. He keeps them on shelves around the classroom and uses them at will. And if, bless you, you have to use the bathroom, he'll make you carry an entire toilet seat as a bathroom pass. I wonder, and hope, that the toilet seat was bought particularly for this use, but I'm afraid it's an old one he brought from home. It disturbs me so much that I restrain my liquid intake prior to his class.

Yesterday, history class ended early, so the teacher flit his hand and told us to chat. I, of course, sat there like a

57

mute slug. But the strange girl (although, despite her strangeness, she *did* have cute clothes), came over and sat at the empty desk in front of me.

"Hi, I'm Heather," she said. She had a voice like a ten-year-old and a face that reminded me of a grandmother. I think it was because she had one of those protruding jaws that old people always have.

"Hi." I said. Of course, she made a comment about how quiet I always am. I swear, I can't get through even one tiny conversation without my lack of conversation being brought up.

"Me and this kid are going to the library after school today. Do you want to go?"

"Uh, sure," I have no idea why I said this. I really, really didn't want to go. Going would have required me to talk, and I probably would have just stared at the books and ignored her anyway.

"Cool! Give me your number and I'll call you." I don't even know why I gave her my number, but I did. I think it's because it was the option that required the least amount of talking.

When the bell rang, I was even more grateful for that day-ending sound than usual.

A couple hours later, when my phone rang, I ignored it.

So today, Heather comes up to me after class while I'm trying to escape through the glass doors of freedom.

"I tried calling you yesterday, but you didn't answer."

Yikes. These are the kinds of situations I usually aim to avoid. Even though awkward stalks me like some cheesy horror-movie villain, I try to do my best at skirting anything with awkward *potential*. If it can be controlled at any moment, I try to control it. Like I do right now. I eye the stairs and see there's not an opening for me to run.

"Really? I didn't hear it. Maybe I gave you the wrong number," I mutter. I realize how incredibly lame that sounds, but I think it's a little better than, "I hate people and kind of wish you would just go away right now." (I *so* wish I was the kind of person who could say that.)

"Do you know Joe?" Aaaaand she keeps talking.

"Uh, no, I don't think so."

"He says you're kind of weird and really quiet." Well, that was nice of Joe.

"Uh, cool," I say. And then I wave a half-effort good-bye and walk away.

A minute later, on my way to my mom's car, I see this kid, Kyle, who's a complete asshole to *everyone*. Each time I hear him talk, he's always making fun of someone. I generally just want to kick him in the groin whenever I look at him. As I walk, I pass by Kyle and his friends; and I hear him say "Look at *that* fat ass." I hope he's talking about someone else, but I'm pretty convinced he's talking about me.

I slam the car door to the van, thankful it's a Friday. My mom looks at me and smiles. I hate how nice she is so much I want to punch the smile right off her perky face. Almost every day after school, I yell at her. She can say one normal phrase, like "I love that shirt," and I'll explode.

"Well, too bad it makes me look effing huge," I'll tell her. "You shouldn't have bought it. I can pick out my own frickin' clothes, *Mom*." That's a usual conversation between us.

Today, right after this guy called me fat, my mom hands me a bag. It says "Cheesecake Factory" on it. I hate, hate, hate nice people.

"Mom, I don't *want* this. You eat it."

"But I got it for you! I know how much you like this."
I look inside the bag and see Godiva chocolate cheesecake, my absolute favorite dessert, or food, in the entire
world. I'd first tried it a few years ago, on a family trip, and
it was like ambrosia in my mouth. But it's got to be at least
5 million calories.

I sigh. I want the cheesecake so bad it hurts. I think of
every excuse to eat it and every excuse not to eat it. My
stomach and mouth hunger for it so badly that they decide
for me. I start eating before we even get home, and I hate,
hate, hate myself.

I need to get skinnier, fast, because I can't handle people
seeing me fat and ugly and pitiful every single day. I can't
handle feeling like I'm being watched and criticized every
second, like some kind of crazy gorilla in a zoo of
teenagers. I'm trapped behind a pane of glass, where
everyone can see, and I *need* to get out. I have a slice of
cheesecake weighing in my stomach, and another day of
tomorrow, looking and feeling like *this*, seems implausible.

I've contemplated moving to Alaska, where everyone

wears huge parkas all the time and covers their bodies with fur pelt after fur pelt. If I could move to the snow-covered plains of Alaska, hiding myself under piles of clothes, I would. I'd turn into an Eskimo and not have to worry about whether my shirt makes me look fat or not.

But Alaska is a long way away.

Chapter 8

"I'LL HAVE SALAD," I TELL THE WAITER. Whew. It's over.

"What?" they ask. They hadn't heard me. I repeat, trying to be louder and hoping my cheeks didn't flame. As many embarrassing moments as I've had in my life, you'd think I'd be a permanent hue of red. Maybe I should give up this whole human thing and go live in "Elmo's World." La, la, la, la.

"What kind of dressing?" he asks. Why do salads have to have dressing? Why can't I be a toddler again so my mom can order for me?

"Uh, ranch?" He writes it down even though I don't really want ranch. I just said it because it was the first thing that popped in my head, and I just wanted to get the whole talking thing over with.

* * *

If I can't even order at a restaurant, how am I expected to travel to Washington, D.C. with a group full of practical strangers? That was one of the first thoughts I'd had after I said goodbye to my dad and sat my seventh-grade butt on the seat of a bus heading straight for D.C.

I had wanted to go on the trip because it would be an "experience." Our school offered all seventh graders the opportunity to see the monuments of D.C. and learn about this and that and blah, blah, blah. This is one of those times where I envisioned the entire trip in my head beforehand, and I imagined myself socializing and being free and adventurous and spontaneous. This was one of the only times I was actually right.

If I hadn't gone, I wouldn't have met Emili, my current best friend, on the eight-hour bus trip. For some reason, we started talking, and for some reason, we couldn't stop.

Emili and I climbed the stairs of the Lincoln

Memorial, and tripped over them, together. I sat in the theater that Abraham Lincoln was shot in and walked across the street to see the bloody pillow he took his last breath on. We drank stale, unsweetened coffee in the mornings with pieces of Godiva desperately dropped in them for flavor. We linked arms and ran around cobblestone walkways, finding an extra arm in a statue and having more fun than I'd had all year. My entire grade figured me to be mute, but there was a kind of anonymity to Washington, D.C. that let me open up. We went to Arlington National Cemetery, and I saw row after row of equally sized, unmarked graves. Every single one of those graves had a story to tell, but they were silenced by cement and dirt. Seeing row after row of place markers, row after row of dead bodies, hit me pretty hard. Each of those people had been living, like me. Maybe they had gone on a field trip when they were younger. Maybe they were bullied in third grade. Maybe they had family problems or drinking problems or shining moments of embarrassment. Maybe they had fears of dying that kept them up at night.

While we were walking up to a statue, a guy handed me a PETA sticker. It had a picture of a tiny baby cartoon chicken on it, and it said "I'm not a nugget." I thought that was a pretty bold statement for a chicken, and I'm pretty sure its ballsy behavior led me to my current state of vegetarianism. I pasted the sticker on the bus window on our ride back, and I like to think it's still there.

Of course, that trip to Washington, D.C. ended before a week had passed. By the time we got home my mouth closed again and I returned to normality. But like the cartoon chicken on that semi-grimy pane of glass, some things just stick. Emili was one of those things.

* * *

When I got back from Washington, I started growing a fondness for walking. Whenever I hung out with Emili, we'd take treks to the coffee shop and back, gorging on caffeine on the way home or cooling off with fruit smoothies. Sometimes I'd go up to a nature reserve and walk around the park, looking at cranes and bald eagles and beavers and deer as I crossed bridges and walked through the woods.

There was just something relaxing about the ease of walking, putting one foot in front of the other until your legs got sore and your heart pumped out your blood while your pores pumped out your sweat. It was such an elementary thing to love, but I did.

My body was the one thing I could control, and every step made me feel alive. When I was outside, walking through trees, I felt wild and free. At least until an airplane flew overhead and brought me back to reality. But until then, I was hippie-ing out and hugging trees being "one with nature." I wanted to keep walking, out of this town and out of this world. I wanted to be Forrest Gump and keep going and going just because *I could*.

It's nice being reminded you're human.

But now I've stopped loving it and started using it instead. I get on the treadmill almost every day and walk a mile just to make me hate myself less. I play episodes of *Gilmore Girls* back-to-back, walking the entire time. I've taken something I loved and turned it into something else. Actually, I've done that with a lot of things this year. Instead of watching a movie just because I want to, I start watching it because it makes two more hours pass by of me not eating. I manage my time and thoughts around calories, and it makes me both happier and sadder than I've been in years.

Chapter 9

LUNCH PERIOD AGAIN. I swear I could get whip-lash from all of my everyday personality changes. I was just being breezy and carefree the other day, and now I'm stuck in this nervous-bunny-rabbit role all over again. I hop on over to my table, knowing a hunter with a rifle is probably waiting.

Julie, my stepsister, isn't here today, but I sit with her friends anyway. I have nowhere else to go. I cross my legs and keep my lips shut.

There's this girl, one of my sister's kind-of friends, that I hate. I don't *like* a lot of people, but there are only a few that I really, truly hate. She's one of them. I had just heard her talking shit about a girl less than five minutes ago in study hall, but she's sitting right next to her now, smiling and acting like her best friend. She's like the two-faced mayor in *The Nightmare Before Christmas*, except not as likeable.

"I hate this table," she randomly says, raging as if she's on steroids. "All of you guys are so *weird*. And you don't even *talk*. Why the hell don't you talk?" She says this last bit to me, gesturing her hand out and scooting back with her chair.

Because I hate you. I'm so tempted to lash out at her, use words to rip down her annoyingly high ego and slap her pale face red. But my mouth stays shut, and I just stare at my folder lying indifferently on the table.

A new semester starts soon, and I really hope my new lunch block excludes her.

* * *

It does, but it also excludes my stepsister. I hover near the edge of the cafeteria, wondering whether to try and find an empty table or bolt to the bathroom.

I spot one of Julie's friends and latch on, yet again climbing closer to awkward.

The whole table is pretty quiet, actually, which makes it even worse.

"Why aren't you eating?" one of the guys asks me.

I mumble something like "I forgot my lunch" or "I'm not hungry." I have a supply of excuses I use when someone notices I'm not eating, and I spit them out unconsciously.

"You're fasting?" he asks. I'm not sure if he thinks that's what I said or if it's a joke. I just shake my head and laugh. Sometimes, I stray so far from normal I wonder why I even try.

Watching everyone eat is both torturous and rewarding. Obviously, when your stomach's growling, it's hard to stare at pizza and chocolate. But I love knowing that the cheerleader eating a biscuit will have to work it off later; and with each chip that girl in my history class puts in her mouth, a tiny ounce of fat has more of a chance of cropping up on her thighs. I feel superior and pathetic at the same time.

Last night, I looked up the height and weight of celebrities, comparing it to the number on my own bathroom scale that tells me I'm fifteen pounds less than when I started the school year. Google calls it "thinspiration" when you head online to stare at models and actors to keep you skinny. The term is clever enough for me to keep googling.

But typing it also led me to all these stupid "self-harm" sites, as if I'm cutting myself or something. I remember when I pretended to have a rash a couple years back to get out of school, and I kept scratching my arm until it was red. And then I *kept* scratching. I scratched until a layer of my skin came off and then I *kept* scratching. It hurt like hell, but I wanted to get out of school so badly that I just kept messing with it. I ended up going to school anyway. Eventually it scabbed over, and I wound up having a scar for months afterward.

But dieting isn't the same as cutting. It's nowhere close. I push my chair out and head to study hall.

I sit down in the first row and this girl sits behind me, bumping my shoulder with her purse and then apologizing. A guy sits in front of me and starts talking to the purse-bumper. I sit silently and doodle.

When the announcements start playing on the TV, as they annoyingly do every study hall, I keep doodling. I feel the guy in front of me turn around in his seat, and I look up at him.

"What day did they say?" he asks.

I just stare at him. I figure he's talking to the girl behind me because, honestly, why would he talk to me when he's already buddy-buddy with purse girl? I keep sitting and staring, as if I belong in the special ed classes. It's too late to interject with a casual "Oh, I don't know" or something that might save him from thinking I'm a complete psycho. Earth, seriously, just swallow me up. When he finally turns around, I look at his back and feel like a complete asshat.

This moment right here? It's the story of my life.

Chapter 10

FOR SOME REASON, I'VE ALWAYS been in love with magic. I think it's because my life was so boring that the surrealism attracted me. I would watch Criss Angel marathons and look online for tricks. I'd practice for hours and pop surprises on my 'rents and siblings whenever I had the chance.

One time, I blew my breath on my mirror and drew a couple of stick figures. When they faded away, I headed to my mom.

"Hey, you," I said, handing her a pad of paper and a pen. "Draw something really fast and easy in five seconds. GO!" Of course, there was always the option she'd draw a flower or something, but out of some fate, she drew a stick figure. Half of successful magic is just plain chance.

I brought her into my room and reflected her drawing in the mirror. The fog had faded and presently, nothing showed but our reflections. When I breathed on the spot I elected as my sketchpad, a cheery stick figure joined our party. She gasped. I smiled. But then she had to ruin my fun.

"You could have just drawn it earlier, before I came in the room," she said. Sometimes, despite being blond, my mom was smart. At that moment, I hated her for it.

She made a smiley face somewhere on the mirror, but when she blew on it, a stick figure popped up. It was one of the few other spots I'd drawn on for practice, and because she didn't fog the mirror before she drew her own artwork, her smiley face didn't stick. But mine sure did. I grinned my big whites and let her think I was Criss Frickin' Angel.

That wasn't the only time my childhood threw magic at me.

When we were younger, my mom took us to one of her work parties. There was a bunch of kid stuff there, and a

DJ who took our kiddie requests very seriously. He was a cool dude, and after a while of chatting with him, he handed us a CD. He was some kind of musician, and because he had a CD, I instantly thought he was famous. I totally bragged about it at school for a couple weeks.

But the main reason I was interested in this party was for the magic show. All of us kids sat in a circle and the magician told us to think of a circus scene. I imagined a clown on a tricycle. He flipped through a coloring book and, lo and behold, there sat a goofy-haired biking fool on page fifteen.

"Who thought of this?" the magician asked. Some other girl raised her hand, and I got seriously mad that she thought the same thing I did. I thought she was lying, and I gave her a lackluster version of my current death glare. Obviously, I've perfected it over the years.

Then, he asked for a volunteer to give him twenty dollars. He put it in his hat and popped out a one dollar bill. If he could do it in reverse, then we'd be in business. He picked my brother to come up and inspect the dollar bill, but he took it and ran as fast as his twelve-year-old feet could carry him. My mom yelled his name, but he just ran in circles and waved that dollar bill high over his head.

Finally, someone caught him and returned Benjamin to the magician. I just laughed because, honestly, it was the best part of the show. You know how when you're a young kid your excitement for something is completely amplified? I was really *ready* for that magic show, and I could easily explain each and every trick he did. The letdown from that buildup is basically my life's anthem.

We left and, on our way out, ran into some Teletubbies dancing. The yellow one with the ridiculous stem sticking out of its head was shimmying with the small, eager purple one. Later, I saw them drinking beer. Sometimes, "childhood" is a very distorted word.

* * *

I have lost all my hope for magic. I was sometimes bitter as a kid, but I used to believe in Santa Claus and the Easter Bunny and the Tooth Fairy. I never questioned how each of them snuck in and out of our various houses during their specific seasons; I just accepted it as magic.

I used to have a religion, and now I'm just confused.

I'm in high school now, and every piece of magic has left.

I wish I could get back some of that childish innocence, back before anything mattered. Way back when I was five or six and the cats at the zoo still seemed exotic to me. Back when I had my mom read *Are You My Mother?* over and over again, and each time was beautiful. I miss that.

Chapter II

"WHAT'S THAT SOUND?" I ASK MY MOM. We all stand and listen for a while. It's a soft fluttering, like leaves rustling or . . .

"A bird!" my mom shouts as we see its wings flapping in the fireplace. "Open the door!" I run over and slide open the glass doors and the bird comes swirling into our living room. We grab brooms, trying to swat it out the door, but it just chirps and dive-bombs us. It's like that Hitchcock movie come to life. I scream and run for cover.

Every window in the house is open, but the house is silent.

"Is it gone?" my brother asks.

"Chirp," the bird responds.

We chase that thing in every room of the house, but it is determined to join our family. Every so often, it turns silent, but then a chirp brings us back into a bird-chasing frenzy.

By early morning, the bird has been silent for a couple hours, but they've been tense hours. During the night, I kept expecting its golden beak to start pecking my eyeballs at any second, but somehow I finally managed to fall asleep.

Once the light of dawn arrives, though, the bird attacks again—by chirping us to death. We swat it out the window, and finally it flies free. My mom and I look at each other, holding our broomsticks, and laugh. Weirder things have happened.

* * *

There are times with my mom that have been good, and there are times with my mom that have been bad. But she's my mom. The way her drinking affected me was real, and it was tough to deal with, but at the end of the day she was my mom and I loved her. Today, she is completely sober, but I still remember my childhood as a routine of hurt and confusion. Neither my life at school nor my life at home was very happy, and part of my childhood was lost because of that.

I always worried about her when I was younger, and as I grew up I still worried. I used to worry she'd get in a car accident and die, leaving me motherless. When I got older, and she got sober, I always worried she'd go back to drinking again. She had tried to quit several times, and that up-and-down, happy-sad upheaval I felt was horribly hard. I worried, worried, worried when I was a kid, and I worry, worry, worry now.

My mom drank too much and fought too much and left too much. Her drinking was so bad that it was like a constant battle to find my mother. When she was drunk, I didn't even recognize her—she was this person who fought and forgot to pick us up and left to go to bars. When she was sober, she was the best mom in the world. She was two people.

And I can't blame her for it. She had post-traumatic stress disorder from a past so horrific that I can't even *imagine* living it. She was self-medicating because life is too freaking hard for anyone to deal with, especially her.

But that doesn't mean I agreed with her poison.

One time when she was drinking, she got in her van and backed out when the garage door was still shut, denting it into some kind of deformed mass of metal. I had begged her to stay, but she tried to leave anyway. Not even taking her *keys* could make her stay since she just up and walked out the front door.

I pictured her walking around aimlessly, getting hit by a car or something. The driver wouldn't see her in the dark, and she'd step out into the street and be flattened like some kind of deer. I imagined cops showing up to tell us she was dead. And that would be the end of my mother.

But she did come back, thanks to some random late-night driver. She had gotten lost in the neighborhood and someone had taken pity on her.

Sometimes, she just didn't show up at all. I remember when I was in fifth grade, I sat on the bench outside of school, the wood uncomfortable on my thighs as I shuffled, waiting. I tried calling home from the payphone, luckily having a couple of quarters in my pocket, but no one picked up. My mom was twenty minutes late.

I had missed a few days of school a week before, so books and pounds of homework were weighing down on my back as I started walking home. It was about two miles, and I wasn't used to grueling exercise back then. I walked and walked and walked. I was sweating through my shirt, and my shoulders ached from the straps of my backpack pulling my shoulder muscles practically down to my ribcage. It was embarrassing. The sidewalk was close to the street, and I knew kids were being driven home from school or soccer practice. I could picture them watching me out of grimy car windows, criticizing me as I tried to keep myself from crying. My brother was at the high school, way too far away to walk, so I had to get home and find a way for him to get picked up, too.

The second I stepped onto our street, the garage door at my house went up. Murphy must really hate me, but his law sure doesn't.

I went over to my mom's van and peeked in. "I walked home from school," I said, which was blatantly obvious.

"I'm sorry," she said, her voice watery and slurred. She'd obviously been drinking. "My alarm didn't go off." I got in the car and we went to pick up Ryan.

"Were you drinking?" I asked her.

"No," she said. "I just took a nap." It was hard to believe her, but I ignored my thoughts and memories as we drove, listening to the music on the radio and nursing my sore shoulders.

We found Ryan as he was starting to walk home, step after step, and we pulled over so he could get in the van. We stopped by McDonald's on the way back and ate greasy cheeseburgers, the bread forming indentations around our fingers.

* * *

During seventh grade, my mom's drinking got really bad—that was when my dad told us we were going to live with him.

My brother and I sat out on the porch steps, waiting for my dad's truck to pull up in the driveway. I felt numb and depressed; I wasn't sure if I wanted to move and get away or stay and submerge. It was this huge decision that meant another school and another house and another life. Change is something welcome, but it's something that's scary as hell to me. I tried to think of something funny to say to my brother as we sat on the steps, but nothing came.

We shuffled into my dad's truck, and I lowered my eyes and picked at my nails as we drove. We stopped at some kind of office, where my dad had to fill out some kind of paperwork. We sat down in stiff chairs while he wrote with one of those pens chained to a clipboard. The managers of the world must be super worried about "Grand Theft Pen."

"Hey, Dad? What about Kringer?" He stopped writing to answer me.

"He's gonna have to live at your mom's." At this, the thought of losing my cat, my eyes betrayed me. I sat in my uncomfortable seat and cried. I was as close to Kringer as any human can be to a cat. He was a smart, clever ol' thing. He knew how to say "hello" and could stand up on his hind legs to turn a door handle and enter a room. He was in my lap every time I was sitting and followed me around every time I wasn't. And, now, I would probably barely see him.

The next day, I didn't go to school. I still had to be withdrawn from my old one and enrolled into my new one. The whole process meant a few days out of school, and I was completely fine with that. I lay on my dad's couch, which I guess could now be considered *my* couch too, and pretended to be semi-happy.

But a couple days later, I was enrolled. And I was supposed to go to school.

"I'm not going," I said. I started to cry and threw a hissy fit, stomping around and saying I had to go to my mom's house. So my dad took me, and they had a talk while I lay on my couch, which I guess could now be considered my *mom's* couch, and pretended I wasn't listening.

My dad being in my mom's house was totally and completely weird. Two parts of my life were meshing; right was wrong, left was right. My world was a complete mess.

* * *

After a couple years living with my dad, I now live with my mom again, back in the ever-perky town of Avon Lake. I've moved a heck of a lot in my life, always envisioning something better than where I moved from. I was always sorely disappointed. Getting used to new people and a new schedule and a new life is a hard adjustment, but I kept moving because I hoped "new" would be an improvement.

Chapter 12

MY TEACHER ENDS HISTORY CLASS EARLY again, damn him. People start talking. I start to feel sorry for my doodling self, so I look over and smile at this girl I used to talk to in, I think, sixth grade. She was on my bus and, for some reason, I've always been more comfortable talking on buses. Maybe the slight chance of danger compels me to speak my mind. Anyway, that was way back when, but today I don't have much potential for new friends.

We start making awkward chitchat, and then the bell finally rings. I grab my backpack and shuffle outside. And, yes, I said backpack. It's totally dorky, but I don't have time to head to my locker in between classes. I have to carry this lard of twenty pounds on my back to almost every classroom. You can see books poking out the side of the black fabric, and it's stuffed so full it looks like something a hiker would carry on his way to Mount Everest. It's just one more reason I hate high school.

I'm proud that I actually talked today, but I don't think the world is. I must have tilted the Earth's axis a little bit by speaking, or maybe I made hell a little chilly with my breath. Either way, I messed with the natural order, and I have to pay. As I head toward the school exit, I slip on the stairs and trip over my shoes in a mass of tangled limbs, landing on my ass and scraping my hands. People are standing all around me, and I hear a few of them laugh. Outstanding people, these classmates. My pants dropped a bit during the fall, and I'm pretty sure everyone behind me is getting a nice view of my ass. My hands sting, the palms burning, and my backbone aches something fierce. Making it to the door is pretty painful, both on the outside and inside, but I try my hardest to pretend like nothing happened.

Remind me never to speak again. Actually, I think my

brain already has that one down. It freezes my mouth for me on its own.

In my lifetime, I have managed to fall down stairs, up stairs, and off the stairs. I've even broken a set of stairs (just the carpet attached to them, but still). My brain and my body are constantly at odds, and they can't seem to come to an agreement. I picture them bickering over a treaty, trying to find some way to work together and utterly failing. Maybe next time, guys. Times like these, dying seems like a great alternative to my embarrassment. But I've had way too many horrified thoughts about death to actually consider it.

* * *

"Hey, is Justin here?" some guy asked, rapping on our back door. I was about eleven years old and very untrusting.

"Yeah, he's downstairs," my brother had told him, after opening the door. The man walked in and strode downstairs like he owned the place. I got this weird vibe from the guy, a creepy feeling tingling up my spine, so I yelled at my brother. "You can't just let anyone in the house, Ryan."

"It's Justin's friend!" he said. I'd never seen the guy, though, so I doubted it.

"Lock the doors!" I heard my brother Justin shout from downstairs, in a very serious, very hurried voice. That pretty much confirmed it.

There was chaos as we all rushed to the sliding door and locked it, double-checking the front door in a panic and wondering what the hell was going on. My brother's girlfriend came running upstairs, hugging me and saying "It's going to be okay" over and over. I didn't know what "it" was, but her tone didn't sound like she believed it. I imagined horror scenes involving guns and blood and yellow police tape, chalky lines drawn on the floor in human shapes. I kept trying to ask her what was going on, but she repeated her mantra over and over.

I remember I was wearing this hideous Pink Panther outfit. (Well, at the time, I thought it was the coolest outfit ever, but looking back on it, all I can do is cringe.) It was black with a pink lining, and the sweatpants were way too short. They stopped around my ankles; and when I sat down, they hiked up even farther.

This girl I barely knew was hugging me and freaking out, repeating the same thing over and over like a broken doll. Something was obviously very, very wrong. Was this guy some kind of axe-wielding murderer? Some Russian mobster aiming to get information? My imagination jumped from theorized idea to panic-ridden, gruesome panoramas. I imagined myself being killed in that stupid Pink Panther outfit, buried in my coffin in black and hot, hot pink. My eleven-year-old mind was convinced I wouldn't survive the day.

My brother came upstairs, and I asked him what was going on, but he was zoned out in that adrenaline-infused fighting stance guys get. I looked out the window and saw the guy Ryan had let in starting to climb the stairs to our porch, crowbar in hand. He had left the house through the basement door and run back to his car for a weapon, Justin told us later, which is when we locked our doors.

My mom leapt up from the chair and started heading toward him, opening the sliding glass door and slamming her feet across the wooden porch. Both of my brothers grabbed her arms and held her back, but she kept trying to move forward. Her jacket sleeve ripped at the armpit and I felt like she should care, but she ignored it. She kept trying to move as her arms were held behind her, and I was scared he'd hit her with his crowbar or attack her in rage.

"Stay the hell away," she yelled at him. Hate and malice spat out of her mouth, and I finally understood what a "scorned mother" looked like. My brothers kept trying to pull her back, but she kept yelling and yelling. I felt almost detached from the whole thing, as if I was watching it from an outsider's perspective. I just wanted it to end so I wouldn't have to be scared for myself and my family.

Eventually, probably after realizing we were going to call the cops, the guy headed down the porch stairs and peeled away in his car as Justin recited the numbers of his license plate over and over. When the police arrived, my brother told them the entire story, start to finish. It involved a lot of questioning, and I stood on the porch and watched, still not sure what had just happened. The whole thing probably only lasted ten minutes, but it was ten minutes of confusion and fear and nerves. The details are unimportant (I found out later it was my brother's girlfriend's ex-boyfriend or something), but the fact that I was shot in the face with a blast of reality was what really mattered to me. I could die. Any second. That's not something an eleven-year-old should realize.

* * *

I wasn't even eleven, though, when I'd witnessed my first death. My dad got us this pet parakeet when we were kids. It was pretty to look at, with these bright orange cheeks and green tail feathers. The bird would walk on your hand, very buddy-buddy-like, but then he'd reach down and peck you. I've never had a good relationship with birds. Maybe it's because I'm a cat person, as my very human-like cat, Kringer, would tell you, so birds hate me by default. Whatever the reason, every time we headed into the bird room at the zoo with a cup of nectar, I would get attacked. I've had those stupid nectar cups stolen from me by birds' beaks more times than I can count.

So when I walked in and saw our parakeet lying at the bottom of his cage, I wasn't very distraught.

"Dad, our bird died," I said in a casual voice.

"What? No he didn't. You'd be crying if he did."

"Yes, he did! He's lying at the bottom of the cage, dead." My dad checked and confirmed our bird's lack-of-living status to my brother and me (which I obviously already knew). We bundled up our parakeet and buried him under a tree root at this local park, which I'm pretty sure is illegal, but whatever.

We used to always go to this same park to fish, my dad standing on the rocks above the water and casting his fishing rod down. Sometimes he'd hand me the rod when a fish was nibbling, and I'd try to reel it up with all my young strength. It was a spot of remembrance.

And even though I hated that bird and his biting beak, I was still sad to see him go. To this day, every time we pass that park, I remember him and his snobby, people-hating attitude. I think I didn't like him because he reminded me too much of myself.

* * *

I think death has as much of a fascination with me as I do with it, because I swear our old house was haunted. And for a girl who is deathly afraid of death, that's not necessarily a good thing. But at the same time, because I always feared death, I kind of have an understanding and familiarity with it. I am enthralled by it. I guess you could say I am morbid.

So when our alarm clocks would go off at 3:00 in the morning, despite us constantly buying new ones or unplugging them, I didn't shy away. And when objects would fall or show up in a different spot, I'd just shrug.

One night, there wasn't even a trace of wind to blame anything on. The weather was nice, and our front door was completely shut with the bolt in place. But, all of a sudden, the door flung open, hit the other side of the wall with a very loud, very bone-chilling thud, and slammed shut again. The little angel we had hanging on the front of our door was tossed all the way across the room, landing on our carpet with a bounce.

Obviously, I ran over to my mom and cried like the little girl I was.

And then one time my mom saw a ghost. She said she saw a little boy walking into the bathroom. Thinking it might be Ryan, my brother, she followed him. But there was no one in the bathroom and my brother was sleeping in his room. Later, the picture frames and knick-knacks we had lying on our sink all fell to the ground in one loud clang.

And then came the scariest part. One night, I woke up and saw a man sitting in my rocking chair, head in his hands, staring at me. He had what I now know is a bullet holster across his shoulder, but I'd never seen one before then. He had long, brown hair and I remember him now just as vividly as when I first saw him. I shut my eyes really tight, scared into shock, and when I opened them a couple seconds later, he was gone. My mom said she had seen the rocking chair moving by itself.

Living in that house gave us some chills every now and then, sure, but it also gave me some stuff to think about. Does life go on after death? Was everything I saw explainable and the rocking chair man just a figment of sleep-deprived imagination? Or were there spirits in our house? And if there were, is every single person just a flicker of soul after they die? Or do only *some* people stay here and others go somewhere else?

I. Have. No. Idea.

Sometimes I wonder if this is all just one giant test. Will I be graded, A through F, based on who I was friends with, whether or not I donate to charities, or how many times I laughed at someone's clothes?

My opinion on religion is very marred, mostly by fear. I'm completely terrified of dying. I don't just want to cease to exist, all of my thoughts turning into nothingness. I don't know what happens when life ends, and that lack of knowledge keeps me awake for long, long nights. I wonder and wonder and wonder, but there's no way that question can be answered for me. So what happens next?

I. Have. No. Idea.

* * *

Part of my fear of death means that I always expect the least from people. Trust isn't something strangers get. I start out with suspicion and, maybe after a couple years of knowing them, I put them on my neutral list. So, of course, gas stations scare the shit out of me.

Have you noticed how many shady people hang out at gas stations? I picture every single one of them as a potential gun-toting bank robber, except maybe the two-year-old toddler in the corner grabbing a lollipop.

I've always feared that some bankrupt dude in holey sweats and a T-shirt with sweat stains will go crazy and shoot the whole place up. And then, boom, the big what-happens-after-death mystery would be solved. But I wouldn't be ready, because I still haven't pieced together all the clues.

It's almost comical, my fright. For instance, I'll be sitting in the car while my mom or dad goes inside to pay for gas. I'll lock the doors and pull out a cell phone, pretending to talk on it so no one will try and kidnap me.

Or, this one time, we were on vacation in Virginia Beach and there was a tornado warning on the news. I immediately dropped down on the carpet, curled up in a little egg-shell shape, and put my arms over my head, like they teach you to do in school. Everyone laughed and told me I could get up, but I stayed that way for a while.

When I look back on that now, I can see the humor in it, but I still get scared. When I ride on a plane or go on a road trip or stay home alone at night or order food from some stupid waiter. Fright will always be a big part of my life.

* * *

Today, I sit in homeroom and think about bombs and school shootings and fires and death, death, death.

Chapter 13

MY DAD WANTS ME TO COME WITH HIM to pick out a ring for my stepmom. It's Christmastime and apparently the grand opening of this jewelry store, so everything's on sale.

I have my hair in some kind of ratty-nest bun on the top of my head, and I'm wearing my dad's Coca-Cola T-shirt, which is about five times too big for me, and these ugly gray sweatpants. Obviously, I didn't want to go anywhere, but my dad said what I was wearing was fine, and I grudgingly got in the car.

When I step inside the jewelry store, I can tell my choice of clothing is an obvious mistake. There are *tons* of people here; they're all dressed up in fancy cocktail dresses, wearing pearls and sipping champagne out of flutes. "Underdressed" is too light of a word to describe my bum-like outfit. I'm ready to grab a cup and start scavenging for spare change.

A hostess comes over and asks us if we want anything to drink.

"Yeah, Chelsea, you want a Coke?" my dad asks, trying not to laugh. I glare at him and politely decline. Imagine being in the fanciest restaurant or party you've ever been to, and then picture yourself in sweats. Horrifying, right?

The second we get back in the truck, I try to be mad. I really do. I put on my glare face and force my eyebrows to look stern, but it's too hilariously funny to keep up.

It's embarrassing. Very, very embarrassing. But I've lived with embarrassing my entire life, and after a while, you've just got to laugh.

* * *

There's this girl I see around school who is by far the most awkward person I've ever encountered. I don't think I'm *that* bad (at least, I damn well hope not), but she reminds me a lot of myself and I relate to her. Every movement she makes is unsure and clumsy. In my eyes, she's a complete grouch, like me, and I see her dive into books, like me. I'm pretty sure she's nearly invisible to everyone else, but I notice her because she's like a carbon copy of my personality. Except not. And possibly because she sits near me in study hall.

I wonder if she goes home and relaxes, like I do, or if she stays wired all day. I wonder if she bakes or draws or reads comic books or makes jewelry.

And then I start to wonder about other people. For instance, does the guy two rows behind me and one seat to the left have a dad who beats him? Does the girl in the right-hand corner of the room go home and write to her brother in the Navy? Does the chick sitting diagonally from me make candles in her spare time?

I start to become fascinated with people's lives in a way I hadn't before. I might even have started to . . . *like* them. The horror.

This new outlook makes everything a little brighter, but I only start to like people in an observant way. I don't want to interact with them (I say this like I'm not a person myself), but maybe there's a little hope that I can, one day. I always prejudge people, but sometimes, every now and then, they surprise me.

* * *

"Emili!" I tap her on the shoulder as I run loops around the edge of the water fountain at Crocker Park. Pennies litter the bottom of the fountain, and I wonder how many wishes were made and broken here. I jump off the edge and we walk over to a bench, talking about guys. I take off my flip-flops and set them next to me, fanning out my toes and letting my feet soak up the sun. I feel like a normal teenage high school girl for once, and it feels *good*.

Some guy in his early twenties walks up to us, smoking a cigarette and puffing out the smoke from his lungs. He's wearing some kind of military uniform, strolling around the shopping plaza solo.

"Watch this," he says. He walks over to the fountain, like he's about to do some kind of mesmerizing circus act, and then heads back to the bench. "Can I trust you guys?"

"Uh, sure," I say. He sets down his wallet and keys right next to us on the bench, taking the cigarette out of his mouth and laying it down. As he walks away, his cigarette rolls over to the side of my sandal and starts burning some of the rubber off of it. I'd feel awkward picking it up and moving it to the side, so I just pretend I don't notice.

He does a handstand, walking on his palms around the edge of the fountain. He stops and does a bow while we laugh, and then he picks up his cigarette and wallet and jumps over the divider, stopping to talk to a couple eating bagels at the café across from us.

I guess *some* people are kind of alright. Even if there's still a burn mark on the side of my sandal.

Moments like these are the reasons why I like life. When I can laugh and smile and see the sun and believe that maybe everything will be all right.

Chapter 14

WHEN I WAS ABOUT TEN, I got a piece of metal in my eye. I'm not exactly sure how it got there, although we theorized it happened when we passed by a construction site. I just knew my eye was bugging the crap out of me. I kept scratching it and scratching it, like my eye had suddenly developed a killer case of chicken pox. I went downstairs and complained to my mom, as I was wont to do.

My mom thought I was just trying to get out of going to bed, but after a while, she noticed a speck of grey. My mom filled a bowl up with water and dropped a penny in the bottom. I had to stick my face in, eyes open, and stare at the penny. It reminded me of when I was a kid and my mom would throw quarters in the pool, making me and my cousins dive in after them. There would always be a state quarter or one with a specific year that would be the "Special Quarter." Whoever found it first won the game, so we'd be holding our breath, swimming to the depths of the shallow end and chlorinating our eyes. Obviously, the penny-in-a-bowl thing wasn't as fun.

When the penny trick didn't work, we ended up having to go to about ten different eye offices and having about twenty tests. At the last doctor, I sat there while they made my eyes goopy with drops of what felt like glue but was really some kind of pain reliever.

The eye doctor told me not to blink as he put some kind of instrument to my eye. Do you know how hard it is to not blink for minutes upon minutes? Pretty hard. I thought he was just looking at my eye, so I figured it wouldn't be too bad if I did. So I blinked a few times.

When I was done, my mom told me I was brave. I thought her comment was pretty random, but then I saw the looks on my mom's and brother's faces. And then they started talking about drilling.

Because, I guess, the doctor wasn't just staring at my eye with the instrument.

He was drilling into it.

At the time, I didn't feel anything because of the eye drops, and I had *no* idea what he was doing. You would think the doctor would have privileged me with this kind of information, considering he was *drilling into my eye*, but I'm kind of glad he didn't. Still, I let my brother and mother think he did. I let them think I was brave. And I let my mom buy me a little treat afterward.

Having someone take care of you is a pretty nice feeling. I should just become an invalid.

A year later when I was about eleven, I was kicking a red balloon around in the house, slamming it around our kitchen and chasing after it. I got down on my hands and knees and knocked it around. It bounced into the living room, and I crawled after it. Something made a pretty disgusting crunching noise, and I felt a sharp sting of pain. I looked down to find a broken mercury thermometer sticking out of my ankle. I screamed. My dad led me into the car and we went straight to the emergency room. I laid my ankle up on the dashboard and bit my lip.

When the doctor put me on the table and planted his scalpel into my ankle, I screamed even louder. I kept trying to stall him, acting as if I had something incredibly important to tell him—possibly the cure for cancer. Not believing me, he continued with what felt like an ankle amputation but somehow ended up as stitches.

When that was done, they sent me to an X-ray machine to make sure all the poisonous mercury was taken out.

And then I let my parents spoil me.

And when I was about twelve, I fell onto something sharp and the skin on my knee peeled up. It was pretty messy. My mom and I went into the bathroom to clean it out, and my brother followed.

"Let me see!" he said. About ten times.

"No! You'll throw up!" I told him. He's always had a weak stomach.

"No I won't! Let me see!"

I showed him. He threw up.

And then I let my mom put a pretty Band-Aid on it

and wait on me for the rest of the day. Because, after all, I couldn't walk.

So, basically, I am a sucker for attention.

* * *

Attention definitely isn't what I'm after when I decide to go vegan and cut animal products out of my diet. Good-bye milk. Good-bye eggs (I've always thought eggs were kind of gross, though, honestly . . . they're like eating chickens' periods). Good-bye food.

When I became a vegetarian about a year ago, it was because I saw this horribly nasty video of a cow being slaughtered. These people poked a hole in the cow's neck to drain out all of its blood while it just *stood* there mooing. It was disgusting. After seeing that, I vowed never to eat a hamburger again. I'm not one of those diehard PETA members who dumps animal blood over celebrities or anything (that's a little too *Carrie*-esque for my tastes), but I decided to start standing up for those animals who still, you know, had that blood *in* them.

But I'm not becoming a vegan for moral reasons. I'm

doing it so I have an excuse not to eat. Not just for myself, even though that's part of the reason. I also decide to do it so *other* people don't expect me to eat. I've done the whole Slim-Fast diet more than a couple of times and the whole "I had a big lunch!" thing, but this seems like the perfect excuse. Whether I'm at a friend's house, a restaurant, or whatever, I can always claim my veganism won't let me eat anything. And if they push it, I'll just eat some fruit or something and be A-OK.

I order some vegan foods online, like nuts and dried fruits and shit. I am going to live off of bird food and hopefully be as small as one someday. I eat almonds for breakfast, almonds for lunch, and cranberries for dinner. It lasts about a week, until my mom gets chocolate-covered cherries.

The box of confections sits taunting me all day. I'm starving, but I ignore my hunger. I revel in it. And then all of a sudden, my hand rips the plastic off the box and shoves one in my mouth before my brain even tells me what it's doing. The chocolate tastes like crap. When you're starving, food always tastes infinitely better to you.

But this chocolate-covered cherry has very little taste, and what taste it does have is syrupy chemicals. I am so mad.

I'm mad at myself. But, more than that, I'm *furious* with that damn cherry. It tempts me for *hours* and when I finally cave, I expect a choco-gasm in my mouth. Instead, it's more like the blueberry-pie stage of Willy Wonka's gum meal. It's just *wrong*. I ate empty calories, and for that, the cherry has to pay.

I go into the bathroom and stick my finger down my throat, but nothing happens. I feel the bumpy ridges at the back of my throat, but it doesn't make me gag like it's supposed to. It's not like I want to become bulimic, but I do want to get rid of that damn cherry. But then I look at myself in the mirror and give up.

Chapter 15

I ALWAYS ATTRACT THE *WEIRDEST* GUYS.
Emili and I are up at Crocker Park again, sitting on a
bench, when some random guy walks up to us. He looks
about seventeen or so, with pale skin and blond hair and
oodles of awkward. I hate being mean to other awkward
people. It's like cannibalism or something. So I try to be
nice. I really do. The key word here is try.

He keeps making small talk with us, like "Hi. What
school do you go to?" and it's pretty obvious he came to
Crocker Park just to pick up chicks.

He's wearing this blazer, like he's all spiffy and stuff,
and his friend/wingman (who not so subtly waits a few
feet back and shuffles his feet), is wearing something very

similar. I can picture blazer-man waking up, calling a friend, elaborating a plot and dress code, and then having his mom drop them off. It's pitiful, and I feel horrible for even thinking it.

"I bet you're wondering why I'm wearing a blazer," the guy says. Oh, so maybe he isn't completely weird. Maybe he just came from some high-end function and he's really just some normal, albeit shy, dude.

"Yeah," I say, and give him a tiny, hopefully unwelcoming, smile. I wait for him to explain why, but he just says, "Oh," and stays silent. And then I feel like a jerk. I wouldn't have said "yeah" unless I thought he had an actual reason. But he doesn't. Why do these awkward moments always have to find me?

I try not to laugh, but I look at Emili, which is a complete mistake. We try so, so hard, but I'm sure the poor fellow caught a smirk or two. I look away from her before I completely lose it.

"Well, our ride's here," I tell him. Our ride isn't here. And, since I said it out of the blue, it's pretty obvious.

"Oh, okay. Can I get your screen name?"

"Noooooo." I say it haphaphazardly, like I feel bad about it. I kind of do. "I don't give it out to strangers." Deeeenied. And then we run away. I'm the cruelest person ever.

And it's not like that was the first time "Awkward" finds me appealing.

Once, in fifth grade, the kid sitting across from me on the bus handed me some weird note that said, "Will you go out with me? Check yes or no." *Really?* I hadn't ever even talked to the kid. I was cynical even at such a young age, too. It would have been easier just to check no and throw the note back at him, but I didn't have a pen. I considered stabbing a hole through it with my finger, but I thought that might be a little *too* vicious.

"I, uh, already have a boyfriend," I had lied. Right.

Or when I was at a concert and some guy came over to tell me his friend thought I was hot, and then asked if I was "single." I said no at the same time Emili said yes. So he called the dude over, and I smiled awkwardly and said hi before doing a complete ninety-degree turn and chatting with Emili about anything I could think of.

It was like I had some kind of radar that made any possible awkward moments slither on over. Obviously, something supernatural was rubbing its maniacal hands together and plotting my next embarrassing moment with increasing amounts of joy. Where are Sam and Dean Winchester from the CW Network's *Supernatural* when you need them?

* * *

Spanish class. Again. This time, it's an oral exam day. Every once in a while, our teacher makes us talk to her in Spanish while the rest of the class does a written assignment in complete silence. It's terrifying. And, when I'm put on the spot, my IQ immediately drops 100 points.

For example, in history class a couple weeks ago, when I was asked this ridiculously simple question—one I knew seconds before I was asked it—I completely forgot the answer. I stared at my teacher, who had obviously gone easy on me, and bit my lip. Then I shrugged my shoulders. The kid in front of me turned around.

"That was the *easiest* question." And, not meaning to

sound harsh, he wasn't the brightest crayon in the box. He told me the answer, and I mentally kicked myself in the head. So, obviously, I generally butcher these Spanish exams. I add vowels where there is supposed to be silence and add silence where there are supposed to be vowels. I throw in la's and el's where there is no need and forget them when there is.

On paper, I can be intelligent, but the real world is an entirely different ball game. One I don't know how to play.

* * *

I get physically sick when I have to do presentations. Literally, physically sick. It's not just nerves that take over my stomach, but full-fledged aches of pain. My hands shake and my lip is bitten raw and my entire day is overshadowed by it.

Like today, I have to do a speech in Spanish. I know my day will go like this:

First period: *Okay, so I have several more classes before I have to go talk. Don't worry about it. Don't worry about it. Don't worry about it.*

Second period: *Shit, that went by faster than I thought it would. Get me out of here! Maybe I should go to the nurse's office and tell her I have a stomachache, but then I'd have to go through the same thing tomorrow. Three more periods left....*

Third period: *I'm starting to shake, going over and over my presentation in my mind. And then I go over it again.*

Fourth period: *Please don't let this class end, please.* This is one of the only times I actually want a class to drag on. My foot starts tapping rapidly on the floor, one of my nervous habits, and I pick my nails. My stomach has turned into a monsoon.

Fifth period: *Oh my God, oh my God, oh my God, oh my God, oh my God.*

Speaking in front of people isn't just nerve-racking; it's an entire process of constant anxiety. Every moment leading up to any kind of communication is filled with fearful thoughts, self-hate, and major criticism. I know even *normal* people hate public speaking, so imagine how *I* feel. I'm guessing the way normal people feel about public speaking is how I feel regularly, when I'm just sitting in a classroom or going out to eat. I always feel like I have to put on a show, and the curtains only close when I'm by myself at home.

But, right now, it's showtime. It's time for the thing I've been mentally preparing for all day: speaking. *Break a leg, Chels.* I grab my notes and head to the front of the class, knowing eyes are following me. I stand at the front, my hands crinkling my paper and my feet shuffling and scuffing along the carpet. The whole room is quiet, so I clear my throat, ready to get this over with, but I make a really weird sound in my attempt and it's super awkward and loud. I just want to get my speech over with, so I trip over my words, one after the other. My teacher tells me to slow down more than once, and I nervously play with my hair until I finish. When I'm done, I run to my seat and breathe a gigantic sigh of relief. And then I start criticizing what I said. Especially my throat clearing.

Chapter 16

WHEN I WAS YOUNGER, IN THIRD GRADE or so, I always felt like I needed to prove myself. Sometimes, I'd pick a persona and try to mirror it, like a parrot who repeats whatever you throw at it. Once, I had a few friends over, Ryan and Ashley, both of whom I didn't really know very well and both of whom I wanted to impress. I was sick of the fact that I only had one friend, and was totally embarrassed by how much of a loner I was. So I invited them over to show everyone how social I could be.

Ashley and I were outside poking a dead bird with a stick when Ryan first got his bright idea. We were going to egg houses. And I agreed with it because I wanted to show everyone how cool I could be.

We crept out into the night, armed with mustard and toilet paper, eggs and flour, coffee grinds, and whatever else our arms could carry. Our landlord, who lived next door, got a dollop of mustard on his welcome mat. Our other neighbors got soap and flour mixed inside their mailboxes, and we even threw some on our front door so we wouldn't look suspicious. We were masterminds.

The people across the street from us got eggs smashed on their classic car, which we quickly felt bad about and went back to wipe off. Our "good" deed ended up biting us in the ass, because while we were wiping it off, the lights in the house turned on and we ran home. The cops showed up across the street and we all laid down in the front room, pretending to be asleep but watching the red and blue lights flashing over our ceiling.

I felt really, really badass.

Today, I make a conscious choice to stop caring. I remember that feeling of boldness from my childhood, and I apply it to my new idea with a firm determination. My "new idea" is to quit school. Not in a high-school-dropout kind of way, but I want to start doing homeschooling—taking classes online. I want to get away from all of this *crap* and all of these *people* and go hide under the blankets. Right now, I'll be bold until I can snuggle back into my shell, because there's really nothing else I can be. My math class doesn't have blankets.

Lately, I've been feeling like I belong in *Dawn of the Dead*, going through the motions of living but reacting like a complete zombie—waking up, going to school, doing homework, going to sleep, waking up, going to school, doing homework, going to sleep, and then waking up again, day after day after day. I just *can't* do it anymore. So I make the choice to stop. I sit in my math classroom, going through the same routine I do every day. My math teacher has this monotone voice that makes math even *more* boring than it is in the first place—a feat I previously thought was impossible. He's one of those meat-and-potato guys who always watches football and tries to be masculine all the time. Paired with the fact that he teaches math, he gets two thumbs down from me.

Every day he stands at the board the entire class period and goes over last night's homework, problem after problem, number after number. And then he assigns more homework. And then he goes over it the next day. And then he assigns more. And so on and so forth. It's the most boring class of the day, and most of the time I just zone out and stare at the back of his balding head or watch the squiggly lines of green marker he makes on the white board.

Last night, I was tired of this class and I was tired of this school and I was tired of caring. So I didn't do my homework. I just quit, and it tasted absolutely fabulous. I'd compare that taste to Sookie's "magic risotto," *Gilmore Girls*-style, with a nice fine wine and a sprinkle of excellence to garnish. When my teacher comes around to check my homework, grade book in hand, I say I didn't do it; he writes a little zero next to my name. I'd skipped out on doing it a couple days ago, too, so I think he's catching on that I'm failing to care. I figure I'll keep getting bad grades until my mom agrees to let me be homeschooled. I never said I wasn't manipulative.

He goes up to the front of the class and is all, "Some of you who've always done your assignments in the past have stopped doing them," with a shake of his head. I feel like his comment is obviously directed at me, and I get very defiant about that. I tap my pencil in an agitated way, but then I realize it draws attention to me, so I quit. I'm good at quitting.

* * *

"I want to be homeschooled, Mom." I just blurt it out randomly, the next day, like I'm not nervous about it at all. But my stomach has tied itself into knots only sailors could master.

"What? Why?"

"I think there's something wrong with me," I tell her, because there is. I don't usually like to get all *mushy*. I'm fine with my feelings staying inside, thank you very much. But I have to tell her how I feel to be able to make this work, so I suck it up and talk brave about goopy, girly, emotional crap.

"What do you mean, there's something *wrong* with you?"

"I don't . . . talk to people, Mom. I just . . . don't."

"You're just shy, honey."

"No, I'm not just *shy*, Mom. I know what being shy means. This isn't normal."

"You're fine. We'll talk about it later." I stomp away and go hide out in my room.

Chapter 17

MY HEART'S RUNNING—SPRINTING, really—at 100 miles an hour; not because I'm alert or anything, like most people who use that expression, but because it's trying to get the heck out of my Spanish classroom.

"We're salsa dancing today," my teacher had said.

Oh, no. See, I don't dance. Ever. Chelsea Rae Swiggett is to klutziness as a figure skater is to gracefulness. I mean, if life were a tangible thing, I would *so* trip over it.

So hearing that I had to dance, for a grade, was basically like saying I had to be tortured by Jack Bauer to pass high school.

Later in the day, all the Spanish classes meet up in the gymnasium to learn how to salsa. It's like two of my most embarrassing subjects joining forces to create one epic moment of sheer mortification for me. And they succeed.

I do the salsa—or at least the tomato part of the salsa. It isn't quite the full thing, but I try, in a shufflelike kind of way. It is mortifying displaying my gracelessness to the public. I'm positive everyone is going to go home and text each other all night about what a fool I am.

I think I must flirt with both extreme self-consciousness and halfhearted narcissism. On one hand, I worry about every single aspect of my looks and thoughts and breathing routine. If there's one flake of nail polish missing on my pinky nail, I'll obsess over it all day, picturing people thinking of me as a slob. If I wear sweatpants to school because I'm way too tired to get dressed, the entire time I just want to get home so I can be away from other people's eyes. And, God forbid, I get a pimple—I'd have to fake sick again. The narcissism part comes from thinking every single person *cares* what I look like. I feel like everyone is watching me and judging me, which makes me feel shallower than a flippin' kiddie pool.

After I do my tomato dance, arms flopping around like

some kind of dying animal, my Spanish teacher utters the second-worst news she could have stated (the first being, obviously, a zombie apocalypse): we have to pair up. With a guy. And I've never met a guy in my entire life that liked tomatoes.

Most people choose their partners based on who they are crushing on, like normal teenagers, while I wander around the gymnasium trying to find a loose tile to hide under.

Eventually a teacher comes over, noticing I don't have a partner, and makes everything even more embarrassing by making a show out of it.

"Who else doesn't have a partner?" she asks out loud, walking around and dragging me along, finally pairing me with this nerdy kid I think I shared a study hall with.

The dance instructor tells us where to put our hands (mine on his shoulders, his on my hips). It's way more awkward than should be legal in any one dose of lifetime.

I sway back and forth with this random guy, looking at everything but his face, wanting to be anywhere but here. The guy I'm dancing with looks off to his left and asks some other guy if he "wants to trade." Way to spring my confidence.

This may seem like just another embarrassing moment for me, albeit a really excruciating one, but it is one on top of many. It's been day after day of trying and trying, and failing and failing. I tried to be social, I tried to be happy, I tried, tried, tried. But as I dance with my reluctant partner, red-faced, I know I don't want to try anymore. The music stops and I walk away and stand to the side, speak a couple words to another mortified girl standing next to me. I'm done dancing.

I'm not happy here, and I haven't been for a while. I just want to go home and have my own personal pity party.

Chapter 18

I CALMLY WALK UPSTAIRS into my room, take a right turn past my bed, head into the closet, shut the door, curl up in a ball, and cry.

And cry.

And cry.

I remember the part in *Alice in Wonderland*, where Alice cries so much her shrunken-size body almost drowns in a river of her own tears. I imagine my closet piling up with teardrops, hitting the roof and seeping through the crack under the door, while I continue to wade at the bottom.

I laugh at the thought, but it's a gurgled, strangled laugh. Tomorrow, I'm supposed to run and jump and pretend I'm normal, like every day at school. But I'm not. I'm the absolute zero of normal. I think, in fact, I might be kind of crazy.

Normality just isn't normal for me. When people talk, I stay silent. When people dance, I sit. When people smile, I frown. There's something really, truly broken in me.

I imagine myself on a factory belt, perky blond dolls being packaged and shipped off. A crane plops my arm on backward, twists my torso to the side, and bangs my head on upside down. I'm packaged and shipped out with the rest, even though my contents are jangled and wrongly meshed together. But the customer still expects the same perfect toy. I wish they could just get a refund.

And then all these doll thoughts make me think of Chucky, and I leave the closet. I lie down on my bed and cry until I fall asleep.

* * *

Shut up, alarm clock. You really, really suck.

I had maybe three or four hours of sleep last night, and I can feel it. This giant glob of fear sits in my stomach, where food's supposed to be. If it's butterflies, they've eaten their fair share of leaves, because at least fifty pounds of raw nerves weigh down in my stomach.

My mom taps on my door to make sure I'm awake, and I grumble something very intellectually. I think it was something along the lines of "uuuugh" paired with "aaaack," and quite possibly "coffee." I basically sounded like a duck, but you can't really expect me to string words together after waking up from a fitful sleep.

"You up?" she asks, like she does every morning.

"No." I tell her. Because I'm not. And I'm not *getting* up. "I don't feel good."

"Chelsea, you have to go to school. You've missed too much already." She says this with a resigned face, like she's sorry that she has to tell me no. My mom has a hard time being strict.

"No," I tell her. Obviously, I don't have those same qualms. We go through the whole push-and-pull thing, but then I blurt out something in desperation.

"I think I have depression," I say, and I want to believe it. I need a medical reason to be broken, because the alternative just makes me more depressed. I listen to her breath ease out of her mouth, curling into the air and stinking up the room with worry. I listen to her question me, call me out of school again, and grow a backbone. I tell her I'm not going to school anymore. She tells me I'm seeing a psychiatrist. I plop back in my bed and stare at my ceiling.

She calls some shrink's office, whisperingly asking me if I care about the sex of my "psychiatrist." I tell her I want a female. I think a higher percentage of males are assholes, and if I'm going to be pouring my feelings into a sippy cup for some shrink, I'd rather they lack a Y chromosome.

She tells me my psychiatrist's name, but I forget within five seconds. I walk upstairs and watch a movie, begging myself to forget everything else, too.

* * *

My new shrink has the ugliest outfit I've ever seen. I always thought lumpy sweaters were a cliché for psychiatrists, but there she was encased in one like it was her frickin' cocoon. I half expected her to morph into a butterfly and flit away. I half hoped for it, too.

She gives me some kind of test, and I answer honestly, setting my snark aside for a rare ten minutes. Do you have trouble sleeping? Check. Are you nervous around people? Check. Are you a freak? Check.

Okay, she didn't actually ask that last question—she might have had some form of personality if she did—but when she tells me I have anxiety, I ask the question of myself.

My mom steps out of the room, and "Lumpy Sweater Lady" (LSL) looks at me. I lose it. Right in front of this stranger in a sweater vest, I become vulnerable. I land on Waterworks with a solid pair of sixes, and she points to a box of tissues.

"Sorry," I say. I feel weak.

When my mom comes back in the room, LSL tells her to take a seat. I always wonder why people have to be advised to take a seat. As if humans don't have the intelligence to understand the use of couches.

"Well, Chelsea said she wanted to do homeschooling. What's your advice on that?" my mom asks.

I think it's pathetic that people have to go to a complete stranger to get advice on their own life decisions. Like some stranger can understand what you feel and think and love and hate.

"Yeah, I think that would be fine," LSL says. My mom barely even considered the option until LSL told her it was okay. Like I didn't know what my own self needed over this lumpy-vested stranger. And then we talked about the weather for a bit, as if she was being paid to detail the Fahrenheit level. She should have just been a meteorologist.

I imagine myself like Harper Lee, being a creative hermit and probably living in some cottage in the woods (with my fifty cats, of course.)

The timer on the counter makes a noise, politely telling me to get the hell out. Its indifferent clicking seems pretty damn rude to me, so I give it a glare as I leave the building. Flurries of snowflakes land on my hair and face, freezing my expression, and my shoes crunch the snow tighter to the earth. Even though the building has a rather boring and plain facade, I feel embarrassed coming out of it. I feel like rainbow lights are shooting from the door, screaming my lack of mental well-being to anyone driving down Walker Road. I glance at the street and tuck my head down.

The snow keeps falling and I watch it frost our windows as we drive home.

Chapter 19

DISORDER (NOUN)—LACK OF ORDER or regular arrangement; confusion.

Anxiety (noun)—distress or uneasiness of mind caused by fear of danger or misfortune.

So basically, I'm scared and confused? So basically, I'm a teenager?

It's a lot easier to accept the word "disorder" than you might think. I already knew I was a little effed up in the noggin, so it's nice to have an excuse. Now I can blame chemicals when I make an ass out of myself. Most people don't have that luxury, at least when they're sober.

The hard part is trying to get others to accept it. At first, my mom and brother just thought I was chronically shy. When I told my mom there was something wrong with me, she didn't believe me.

"Hey ma, there's something wrong with me," I had said. Probably not the most tactful approach, but I didn't have much to work with.

But I couldn't really blame them for not getting it. They barely ever saw me outside of the house. They didn't see what I was like around strangers—a tongue-tied idiot, incapable of expressing more than a halfhearted shrug. I think my family had a harder time accepting it than I did.

Stage One—Denial. As in: There's nothing wrong with you. You're just shy!

Stage Two—Depression. As in: My daughter/sister/friend is a nutcase.

Stage Three—Anger. As in: You *will* go to school and you *will* be a normal girl.

Stage Four—Acceptance. As in: Okay, do what you gotta do, chickadee.

I don't think anyone in my family really understood, but they accepted that I understood. And what I understood was that school was kicking my ass, and I needed to quit.

Obviously, I knew that quitting school entirely would probably result in a job at McDonald's, so I asked for the next best option: to take classes online. I felt like one of those übergeeks who spend their entire life on the Internet (more than likely ending up in their mother's basements at age forty), but to me it was easier than facing reality.

I'll procrastinate living in the "real world" for as long as I can. It's overrated, anyway.

* * *

Of course, putting my plan into action isn't that easy. Is it *ever* that easy?

It's supposed to take about three or four days before I can enroll online and, until then, I have to go to regular school. But I think someone upstairs likes me, because the most miraculous thing happened last night.

It snowed. And it snowed. And it snowed.

The sky was relentless, refusing to let one stray blade of grass sprout through the ever-growing mound of white fluff taking over Avon Lake.

I've always loved snow. I love the smell of it and the

bundling of warm clothes. I love when we have a fire going in the fireplace and Christmas lights shining down our street at night. I love the smells, the sights, the sounds, the cold, and the taste of winter.

My birthday is right before Christmas, and when I was younger, I thought all the holiday cheer was just for me. I think it's created a lasting effect, because every December I get this crazy type of glee.

But I'm not feeling the winter spirit at the moment. I'm grumpy and grouchy, listening to the Beatles in my room and feeling like the most angst-filled teenager to walk the planet. Holden Caulfield, you have nothing on me.

The snow piles up so high that my school calls in a snow day. And then they call another one. And then, since the pipes froze and then cracked (and the school subsequently flooded with water), we get *another* day off. And then I am enrolled in the new school.

It's creepy. I tell the world I need a break and it obliges. I think that's the first time the world has ever listened to me, despite how many times I bitch at it. Good job, world. You got one right.

I don't go back to school after that.

Chapter 20

THERE ARE FEW PEOPLE I really look up to; I don't admire any divas or celebrity icons, and I've never met anyone inspiring enough that I actually want to model myself after them. That's probably because I'm extremely judgmental and critical, but it's true.

But author Laurie Halse Anderson is my *idol*. She immersed me in stories and allowed me to be caught up in worlds that were deep, meaningful, and emotional. A world that wasn't my own. I read *Speak* and *Catalyst* and *Fever 1793* and every single book of hers I could possibly get my hands on. She got me interested in reading with more zest than any other author was able to do.

And now she's having a signing. And I, amazingly, am able to go.

I'd spent the past couple years, out of school, reviewing books. I'd finally found something I loved to do—it had been in front of my face my entire life, when I'd carry milk crates of books around before I could even read, but I had never acknowledged it. But as I read and wrote and branched out online, I found a lot of other readers and writers who were as passionate about reading and writing as I was and am. People like me. It was easy talking to people with distance between us and computer screens as our faces.

We drive down to Chicago, my family and Emili and I, stopping to pick up my friend Kristi (who I actually met through the book reviewing world) on the way. The highway makes me think of death, like always, but I'm simultaneously talking about books and life. Thinking about dying and talking about people's lives must seem like an oxymoron, but it distracts me enough to neutralize my fear.

We head to the American Library Association's (ALA) annual event, planning on meeting many of the writers and readers I've talked to online. Actual people, flesh and blood. It's much less terrifying talking to someone with a keyboard, but I'd probably get a few glares if I carried one around in public places.

When we get to ALA, I'm convinced I'm in heaven. I remember reading *The Lovely Bones* by Alice Sebold; in it, every person has a different heaven depending on their passions and interests and dreams. I'd always imagined mine would be a library, one with a never-ending supply of books and coffee. But I was wrong. My heaven is ALA.

Books and their authors are everywhere, signing and chatting. Every single person in this great big building loves books and I love every single person in this great big building.

But I'd spent so much time avoiding people that the idea of intentionally seeking them out is mind-numbing. It's like a hermit crab abandoning its shell and hanging out with lobsters. I generally feel out of place among people, but even though the crowd is large and varied, I actually feel like I fit in. These people love what I love, and I feel less like an out-of-shell hermit and more like a human being.

I am still terrified, thinking people will see me as too young or too inexperienced or too unprofessional. But then I stop thinking and start seeing. I see people, charming and intelligent and funny. I hear conversations, ones I'd actually want to join into. I see books, books, books, and I see what I want my future to be like. I see something I wanted to be a part of.

In line for an author signing, we meet a woman who teaches Young Adult literature and we chat with her, casually, about books and authors and writing and plots and characters. I had never before talked to a stranger so comfortably and assuredly. I know what to say, for once, and I say it. I speak about what I think and I don't think as much about what I speak. I feel like myself in a group of people, and it's a first.

Laurie Halse Anderson, coincidentally, is doing a signing at a nearby bookstore after ALA. Not coincidentally, I am going to be there.

ALA was *a lot* of fun. But meeting Laurie Halse Anderson is different than the whirlwind heaven that was ALA. I'm going to be meeting the person who basically kindled my love for reading, who created it. She made this entire passion of mine possible. And if there's one thing I could ever inspire in someone with my words, it would be to find themselves and what they love and never, ever, no matter what anyone says, give up on it. Unless you love killing people or something. But I, fortunately, don't. I love reading and writing. And Laurie Halse Anderson seemed to be the one to show that to me, unbeknownst to her.

I walk into the bookstore and see LHA with her cheetah-print shoes and cheerful smile and energetic passion and almost have a heart attack. I wait in line, nervously, thinking and thinking about what to say to her. Shouting out "You're my idol!" would probably convince her that I'm mentally unstable and/or a stalker. So would "I love you!" and various other forms of psychotic praise going through my mind. What do you say when you come face-to-face with someone you basically worship? What would you say to Buddha or Zeus or God, had you met them on a street corner?

I can't even speak a word to her when she signs my books. I'm meeting this hugely influential person—

someone who has changed my life—and I can't do anything but grin.

Well, *I* feel like an idiot. Every moment leading up to facing her was full of anticipation, but when I actually get face-to-face, I freeze and shove my book onto the table. Why am I so socially retarded?

But then I see the inscription she signed in every copy of *Speak*, the very first book I read by her, and I feel warm and inspired and *happy*. I feel like her words are jumping straight from the page and speaking right to my heart, as corny as that sounds. The night, the air, the people—all of it is suddenly valuable to me. Time stops out on that sidewalk in Chicago while I'm reading her words. The bookstore we just left lights up the pages and the air feels solid enough to eat. Life can majorly suck sometimes but, right now, I feel like it's worth living. More than worth it.

"Speak Up!" she wrote.

I let it sink in and close my eyes, savoring each precious gold-dipped word. *I think I might have to do just that.*

Epilogue

I'M EIGHTEEN YEARS OLD NOW, and I'm planning on starting college next year. I still have anxiety and I still constantly worry about how I look. I still think about death and I still get insanely nervous when I speak to people. I worry, all the time, about everything. But I've learned to acknowledge that worry and kick it in the ass. I'm living.

Doing homeschooling helped me a lot, even though I wonder how much different my life would be if I'd stayed in high school. I'd be telling a much different tale, I'm sure, but I like the person I am now and the time I spent alone made me realize that. It gave me time to find out who I am instead of worrying about who people wanted me to be. I wish everyone could have the opportunity to sit back and realize what makes them truly happy, and then go for it. I sure did.

I'm still best friends with Emili. She's one of the only people that I can really *talk* to. Without her, I probably would have lost the little specks of brain I still possess. She lets me tell her about all my crazy book plotting ideas and issues (I'm sure she thinks I have schizophrenia, talking about all my fictional characters as if they live and breathe) without batting an eyelash. I think everyone needs a friend like that—one who witnesses your insanity and then tries to salvage whatever's left of your sense. Someone who's just *there*, in the best possible use of the word.

I started working, first as a dining assistant at a nursing home for a total of (I think) three days—I quickly realized that any kind of waitressing/quick-on-your-feet job is probably best for those who don't spill everything within a five-foot radius—and then as a receptionist. I'm hoping to find a job at a bookstore or a coffee shop, where I can spend my entire paycheck on the exact thing I sell all day. That might defeat the purpose, but purposes are overrated anyway.

I've been doing some traveling, even venturing onto a

six-hour plane ride by myself. (I grabbed onto the sides of the seat in a death-grip the entire way, but I made it.) I've been to San Francisco and Chicago and Cincinnati and Louisville and New York and here and there and, hopefully in my lifetime, everywhere.

Learning to drive was definitely an experience, full of shouts and sweat and nervous whistling. But I got behind the wheel and drove. I might have hit a curb or two (or seven), but, hey, my wheels like the feel of grass.

It's easier to talk to people now. I'm still insanely shy and I still mumble and avert my eyes, but I actually speak. I have to force myself to, sometimes, but I do. And, surprisingly, most people are a lot less scary than I'd thought they'd be.

If someone doesn't like what I say or how I act or what I wear, it's their problem. I won't change who I am for anyone now.

I still do embarrassing things, like tripping down (and up) stairs or having my shirt drink my coffee instead of my mouth. It happens. But I've learned to befriend embarrassment. I've learned to shrug.

I've been doing things and seeing things and speaking

and having fun. I still have anxiety, but it doesn't have *me* anymore.

I don't know where the hell my life will take me in the next few years, but I know I'll live it for as long and as loudly as I can.

Book Club Discussion Questions for HANNAH

1. Most teens feel anxious or awkward at some point in their lives. What makes Rae's anxiety different from typical teen angst?

2. Were you aware that severe anxiety disorder was an actual diagnosis among teens before reading this book? Having read about Rae's experience in school, can you think of students at your school who might suffer from the same kind of thing?

3. Have you ever been worried that something was seriously wrong with you, but you were too afraid to talk to someone about it or ask for help because you weren't sure you wanted to know the truth? If so, did you ever get the help you needed? What was the outcome of the situation?

4. Rae spends a lot of time fearing life itself. What kind

of things do you fear that keep you up at night? Are they rational or irrational fears? How do you deal with your fears?

5. Rae writes about vivid childhood memories—the death of her pet bird, a scary encounter with an intruder, long car rides to Ocean City, New Jersey. What are some of your pivotal childhood memories that play a role in defining the person you are today?

6. Rae talks about a trip she took to Washington DC where she was able to make a strong friendship connection and uncharacteristically break out of her shell. Yet, once she returned home, she went back to being her withdrawn, quiet self. Why do you think this is?

7. Do you think today's teens have more anxiety disorders than in generations past? If so, why? Do you believe life for teenagers is more stressful today than it was ten, twenty, or thirty years ago? Why or why not?

8. Rae uses a lot of metaphors and vivid imagery in her writing. How do you think her creative use of language impacts her storytelling and brings it to life?

About the Author

Chelsea Rae Swiggett is eighteen years old and will soon be heading to college to major in English and immerse herself even further into the world of books and writing. She currently serves on the Ypulse Youth Advisory Board.

More Louder Than Words Stories

Code 5283 • Paperback • $7.95

Hannah Westberg has gone through more trauma in her eighteen years than many people will experience in a lifetime. Stemming from her depression and recently diagnosed borderline personality disorder, Hannah has engaged in dangerous behavior and has paid a high price. By the time she was in eighth grade, Hannah was cutting, popping pills, skipping class, and drinking. The following summer, she tried to commit suicide for the first time. Since then, she has had stints in the psych ward, worked with numerous therapists, gone on anti-depressants, and gotten better, only to slip up and relapse, repeating the whole cycle again.

www.louderthanwordsbooks.com

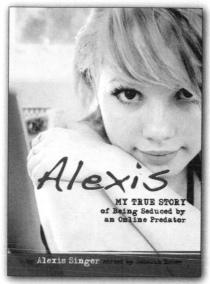

More Louder Than Words Stories

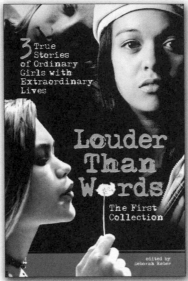

Code 5461 • Paperback • $9.95

Louder Than Words: The First Collection is now three books in one! Fans of the series can enjoy the true remarkable stories of *Marni, Emily*, and *Chelsey*. There's **Marni**, who brings us inside her secret world of 'pulling' and the challenges of surviving high school while trying to hide an obscure stress disorder. Then there's **Emily**, who takes us through the senior year that wasn't when chronic illness forced her to miss out on one of the most important times of her life. And then there's **Chelsey**, who used writing as a way to recover from experiencing the unthinkable when her father was murdered the week before her fourteenth birthday.

www.louderthanwordsbooks.com

Available wherever books are sold
To order direct: Telephone (800) 441-5569 • www.hcibooks.com
Prices do not include shipping and handling. Your response code is LTW.